The Handwriting Patch

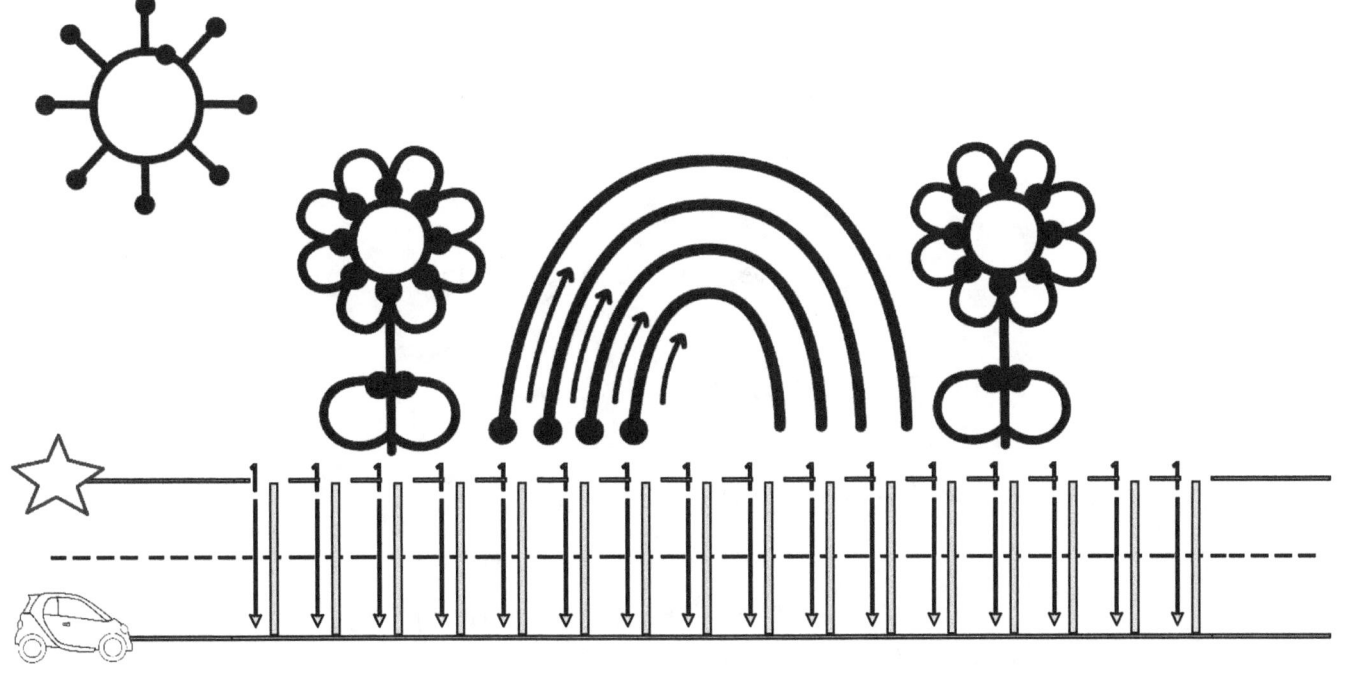

Handwriting Workbook with
fun Step by Step Instructions

Students learn handwriting
while learning to draw

HandwritingPatch.com

For....

Patrick,
Maddie, Karle, Kevin,
Brendan, Meggie, Joseph

For Mom and Dad
And all the Karles and Mousaws

To God be the Glory!

In God Alone there is rest for my soul.
From Him comes my safety.
He is my rock, my shelter, my fortress...
I can never fail.
Psalm 62:1

Learn more handwriting tricks at: HandwritingPatch.com

Help your new or struggling reader at
Reading-Patch.com

As you learn to write, you will also learn to draw.

Have you ever heard of a patch of flowers? Sometimes when you are walking along the road or driving, you see lots of flowers growing. This is called a flower patch. We are going to learn how to draw and write a writing patch!

Here is a writing patch that you can color. Color the writing patch.

Look at the writing patch above, do you see the lines below the flowers? These are writing lines.

When we learn to write, we learn to write on writing lines. Here are what writing lines look like.

The writing lines look like a street! We have to keep a space in between each car so we don't bump each other. Look, there are cars on the street.

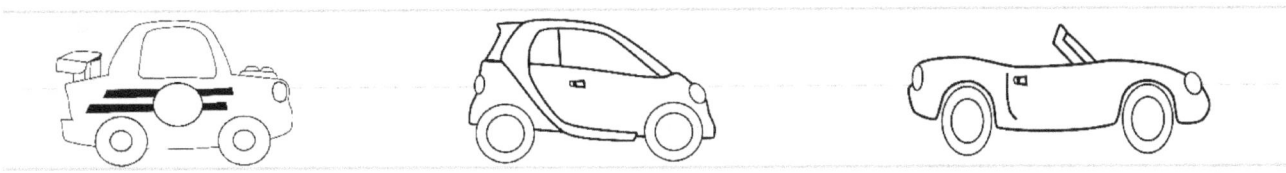

Look! All the cars drive the same direction on the writing lines. Put your finger on the dot and follow the arrow from left to right. This is the direction that the cars drive. This is the direction we write. We start on the left and move to the right.

We are going to call the writing lines the WRITING ROADWAY. Always move from left to right on the writing roadway. To help you remember the direction that we write, look at the car on the roadway. Point to the car now. The car looks like it will drive to the right.

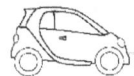

Practice driving a car from left to right on the writing roadway. Find a toy car and drive it on the writing roadway. Remember to drive from left to right!

Now we are ready to learn to write!

Learning to draw and learning to write is fun!

When you start to write letters, or draw pictures in this book, you will sometimes see a box that looks like this:

These pictures remind you of different ways you can practice making your letters. To practice your letters you can....

 Swipe with your finger on your paper.

 Draw the letter in the air with your hand.

 Build the letter with.....
        Playdough
        Write it in Rice, sand, salt
        Write it in shaving cream
        Write it in pudding
        Paint the letter

You want to feel the letter in many different ways before you write it!

First we are going to learn how to draw a seed in our writing patch.

Seed looks like this:

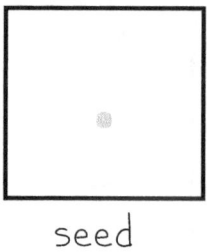
seed

To make a seed, hold your pencil and dot the paper with the tip of the pencil. You can dot the seed here.

seed

Continue on the following pages for more practice.

Seed

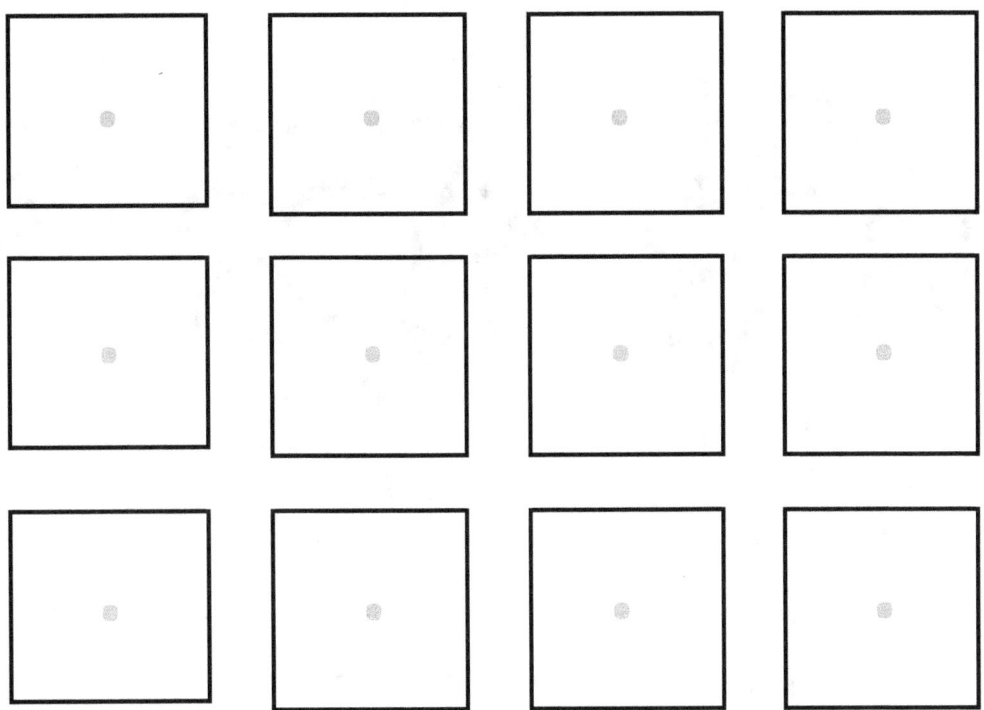

Plant the seeds.

Plant more seeds in the writing patch.

Draw your own writing patch.

seed

Next we will learn to draw grass in our writing patch.

Grass looks like this:

grass

To make grass, you will start at the top and make a straight line down. Do you see the arrow along the line? The arrow shows you that you will draw a straight line down.

grass

Here is a different picture that shows you how you make grass. When you see a picture like this, you can practice making the stroke by swiping and using your finger. You will always start with your finger on the big black dot and follow the seeds that dot the picture. Always follow the seeds in the direction of the arrow. Practice making grass by swiping the picture.

Grass

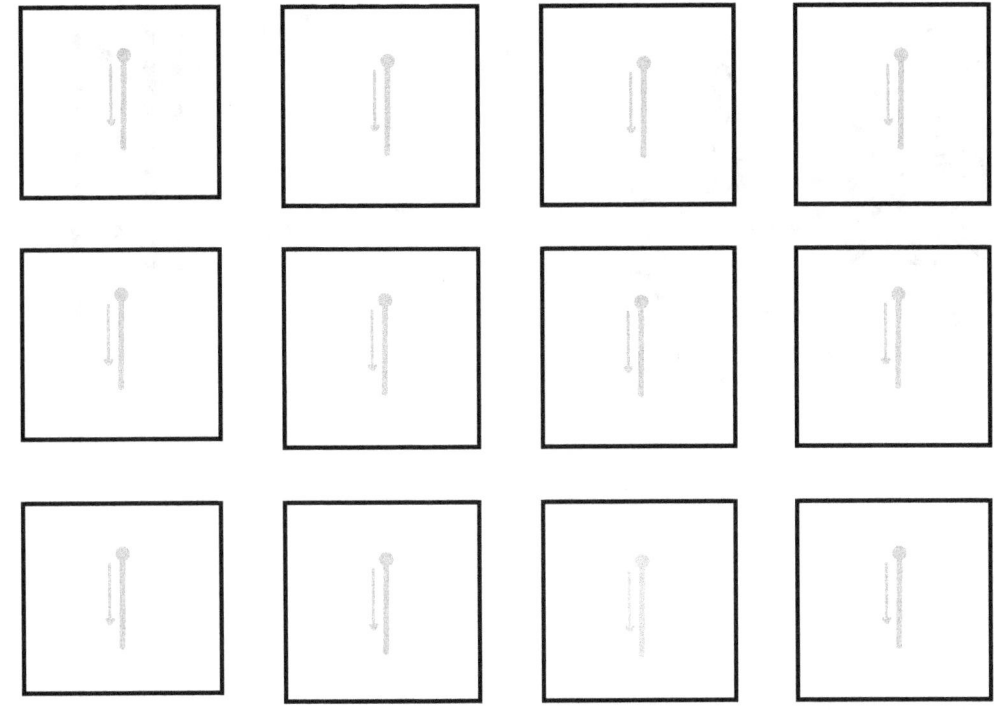

Make grass and seed.

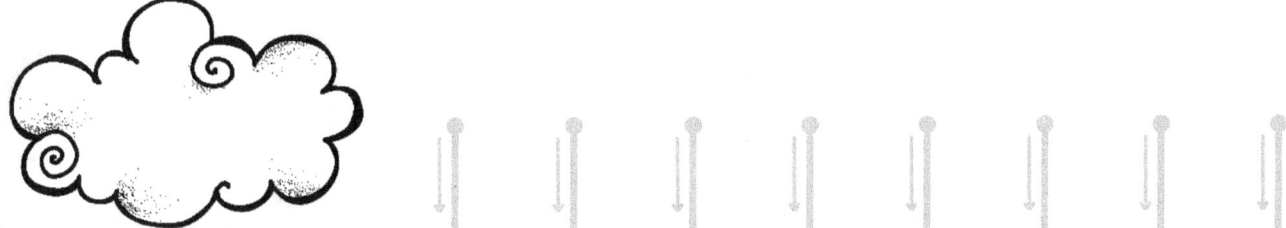

Time to cut the grass.

Draw your own writing patch.

seed   grass

When we write letters, sometimes we begin at the top of the writing roadway. Do you see the star? Point to the star on each writing roadway.

I will say "start at the star" if I want you to start writing your letters on that top line. All capital or big letters start on the star line. Start at the star and draw grass.

Now we will learn to write the lower case letter 'l'. Here is the box that shows you how to write the lower case letter l.

grass

The star in the corner shows you that you will start at the star line. Even though it is a lower case letter, it starts on the star line. Start at the star line and draw grass down to the car line. You are writing the lower case letter 'l'.

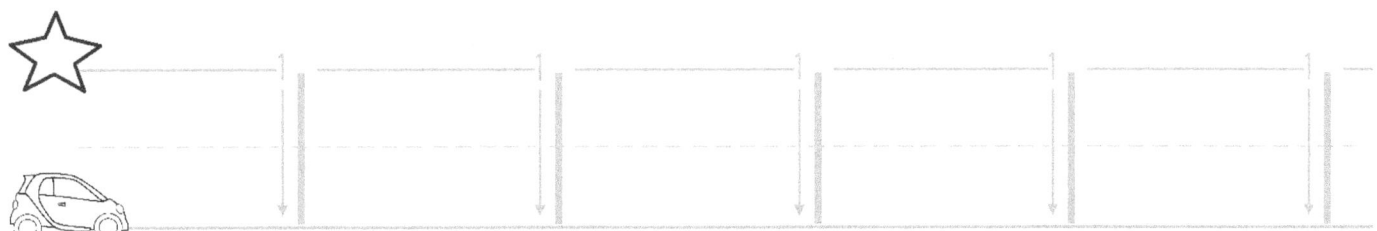

Practice swiping the stroke with your finger. Start at the large black dot, follow the seeds down in the direction of the arrow. You just swiped the lower case letter 'l'.

Continue to the following page for more practice.

Letter l

lion

grass

Teacher Tip!

1. ALL upper case will start on the star line.

2. Only 5 lower case letters start on the star line, otherwise lower case letters start on the dotted middle line. (The 5 letters are b, f, h, k, l)

If the student struggles where to start writing the letter, ask the student if they are drawing an upper case letter or a lower case letter.

All upper case letters start on the star line.

Most lower case letters start on the middle dotted line.

Many students are just learning to read and don't know if they are writing a capital or lower case letter. Once they begin to understand this concept, help them understand that all capital letters will start on the star line and most lower case letters start on the middle dotted line.

When we write lower case letters, we almost always start on the middle dotted line. When I want you to start on the middle dotted line, I will say "Start on the middle dotted line."

Let's learn to write the lower case letter i. The lower case letter i, looks like this: The lower case letter I is a lower case letter so it starts on the middle dotted line.

i

You will use these two handwriting strokes to write the lower case letter i.

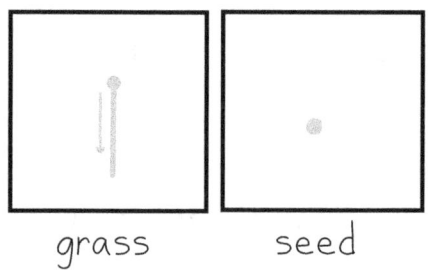

grass   seed

Practice swiping the strokes. Start at the large black dot, follow the seeds down in the direction of the arrow. Dot with seed.

Continue to the following page for more practice.

Letter i

inchworm
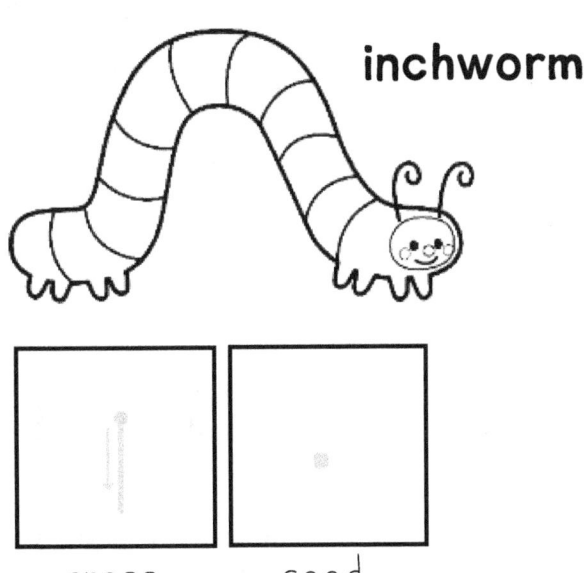

grass   seed

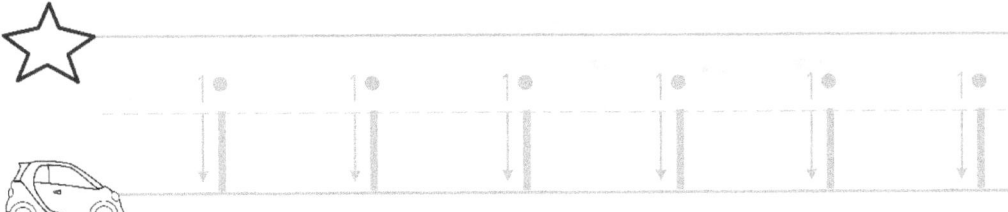

Now we will learn the airplane handwriting stroke.

The airplane handwriting stroke looks like this:

airplane

The airplane swipe looks like this.

Practice swiping the strokes. Start at the large black dot, follow the seeds down in the direction of the arrow..

Continue to the following page for more practice.

Airplane

Make airplanes and grass.

Fly like an airplane.

Draw your own writing patch.

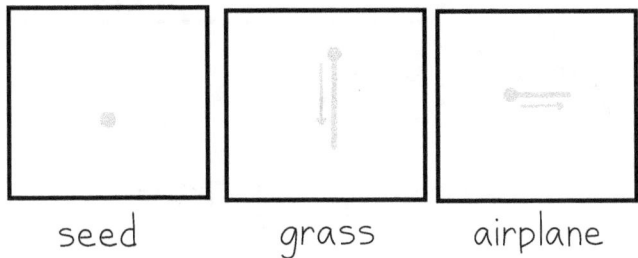

seed   grass   airplane

Letter t

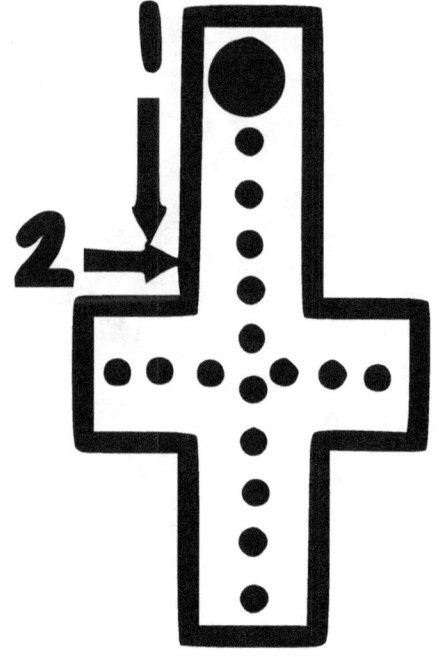

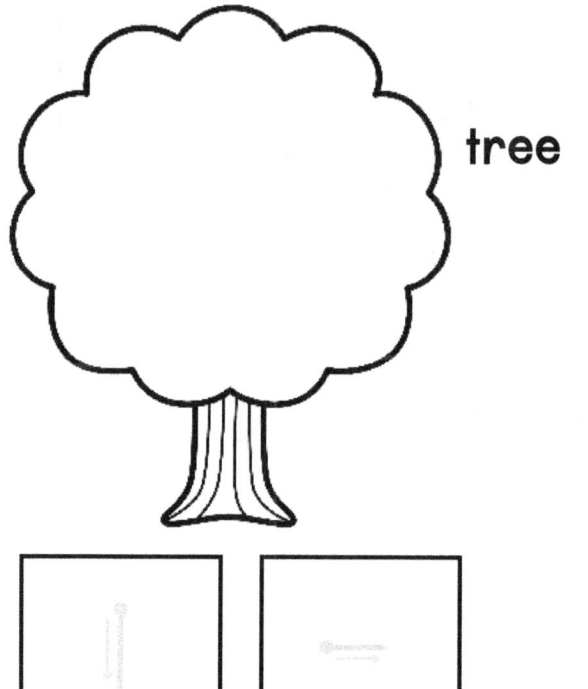

tree

grass   airplane

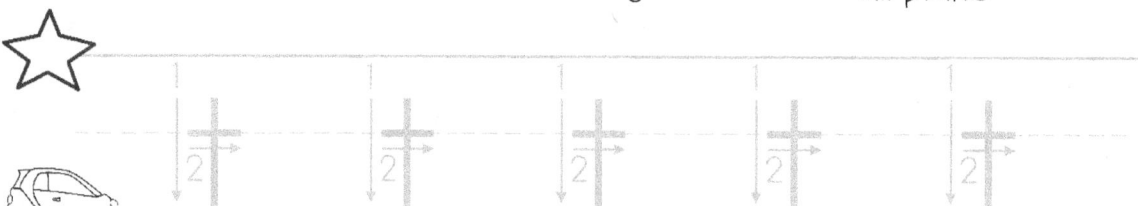

Letter T

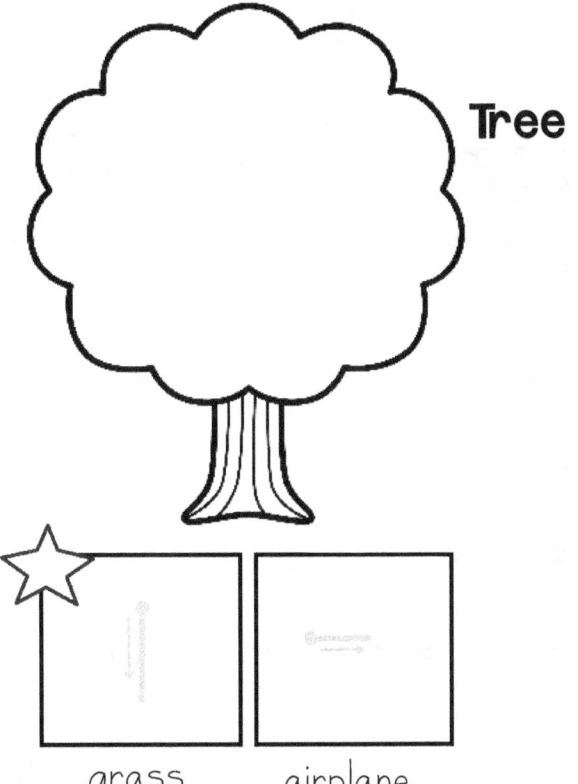

Tree

grass   airplane

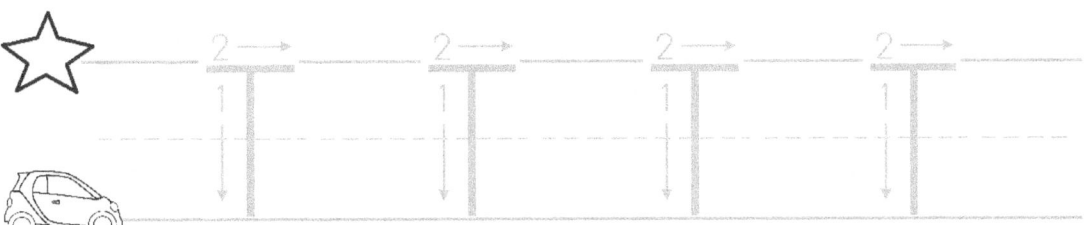

Letter L

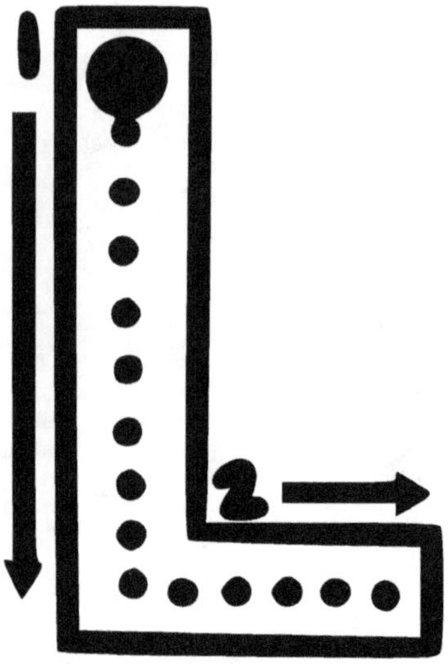

Lion

grass   airplane

Letter E

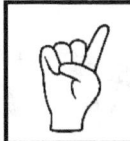  

Elephant

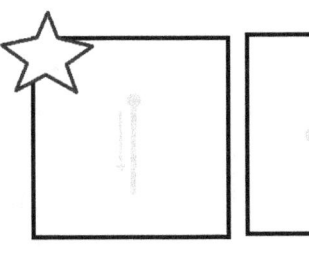

grass

airplane   airplane   airplane

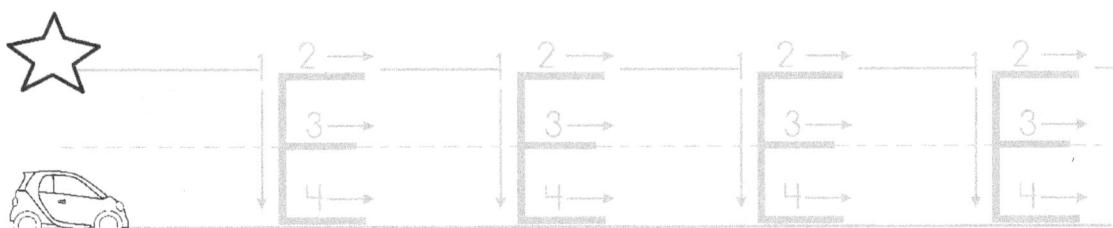

Letter F

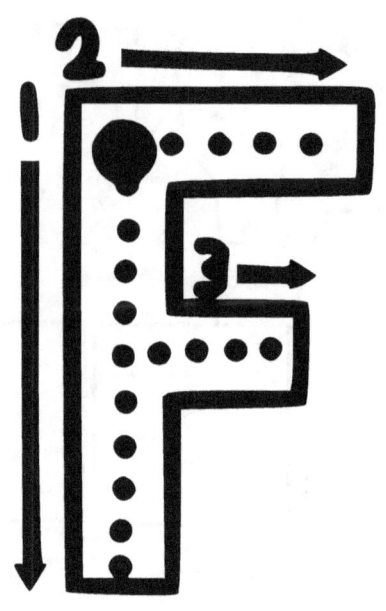

Frog

grass   airplane   airplane

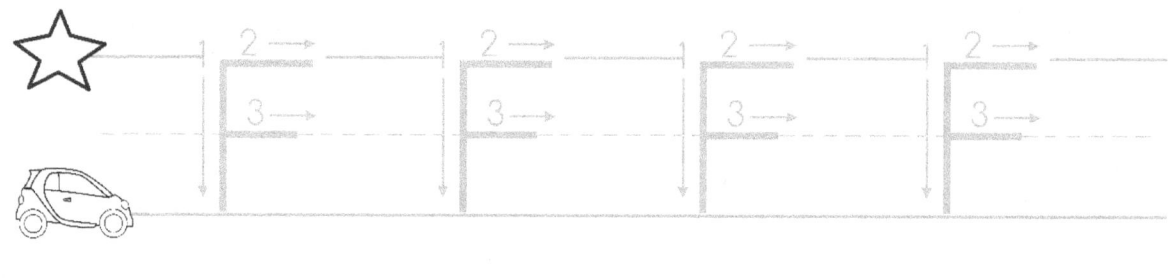

Letter H

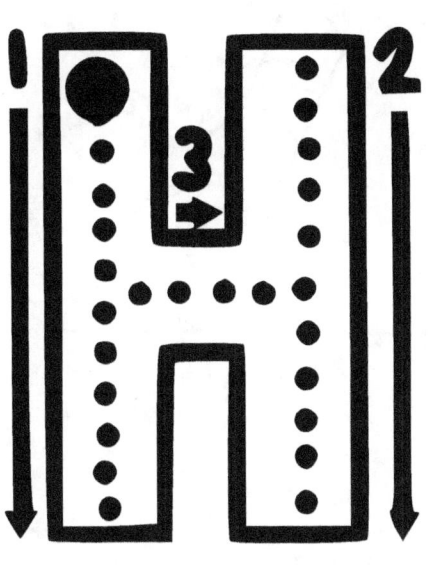

Helicopter

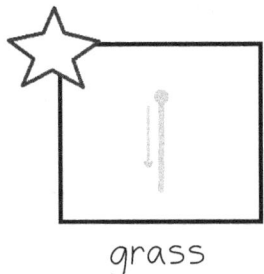 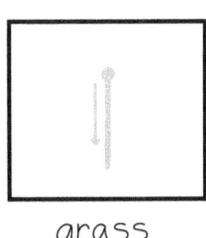 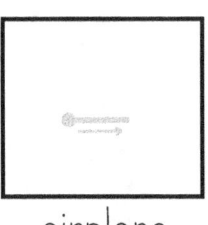

grass   grass   airplane

 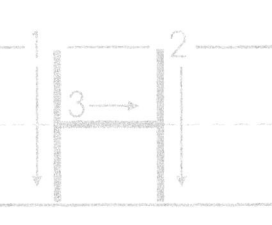 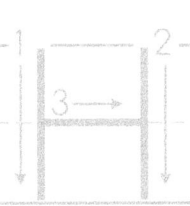 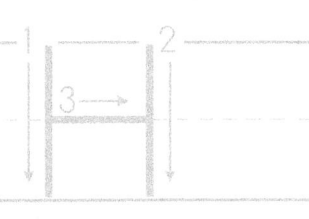

 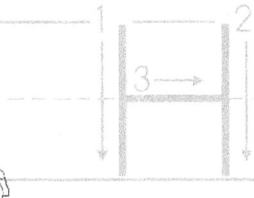

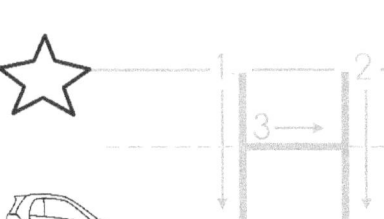

Letter I

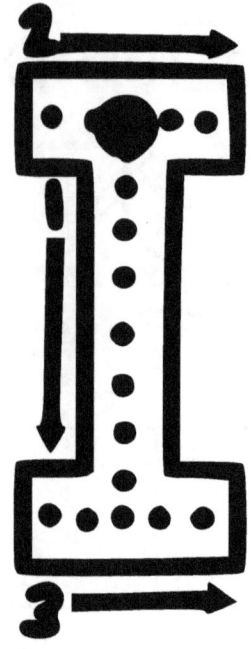

inchworm
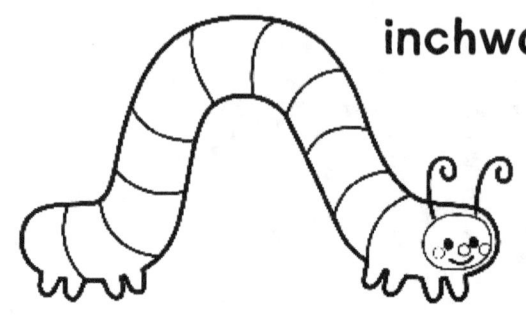

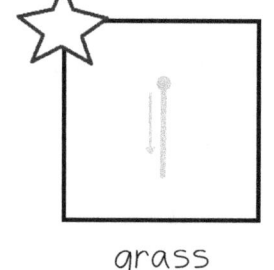  

grass   airplane   airplane

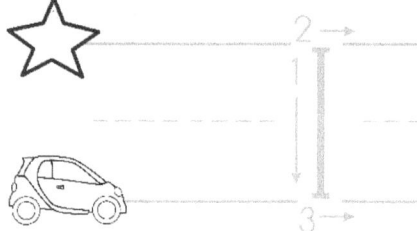 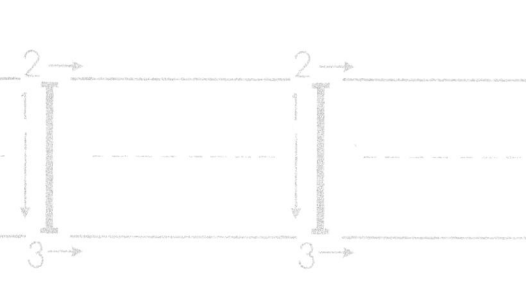

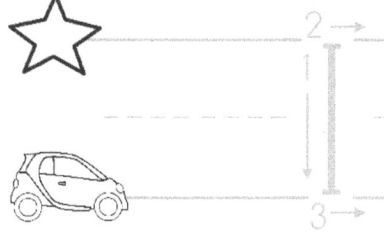

Rain

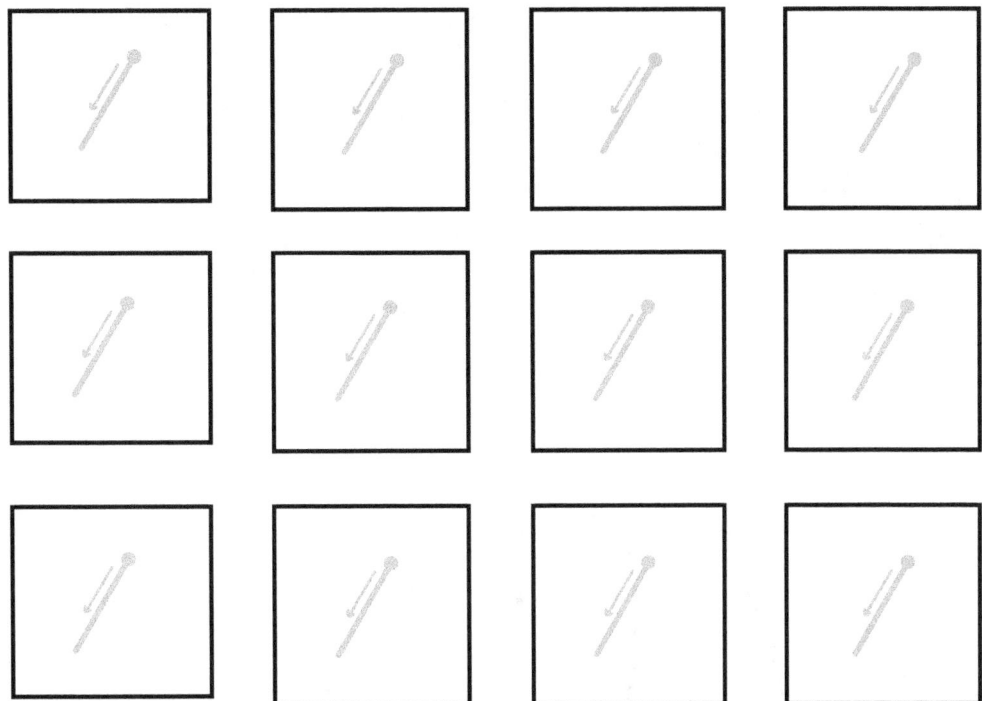

Make it rain.

Play in the rain!

Draw your own writing patch.

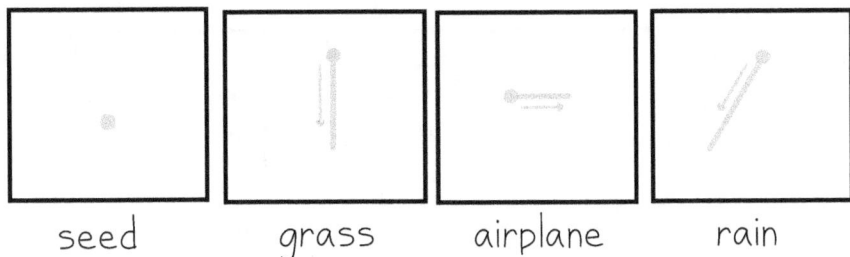

   seed   grass   airplane   rain

Shooting Star

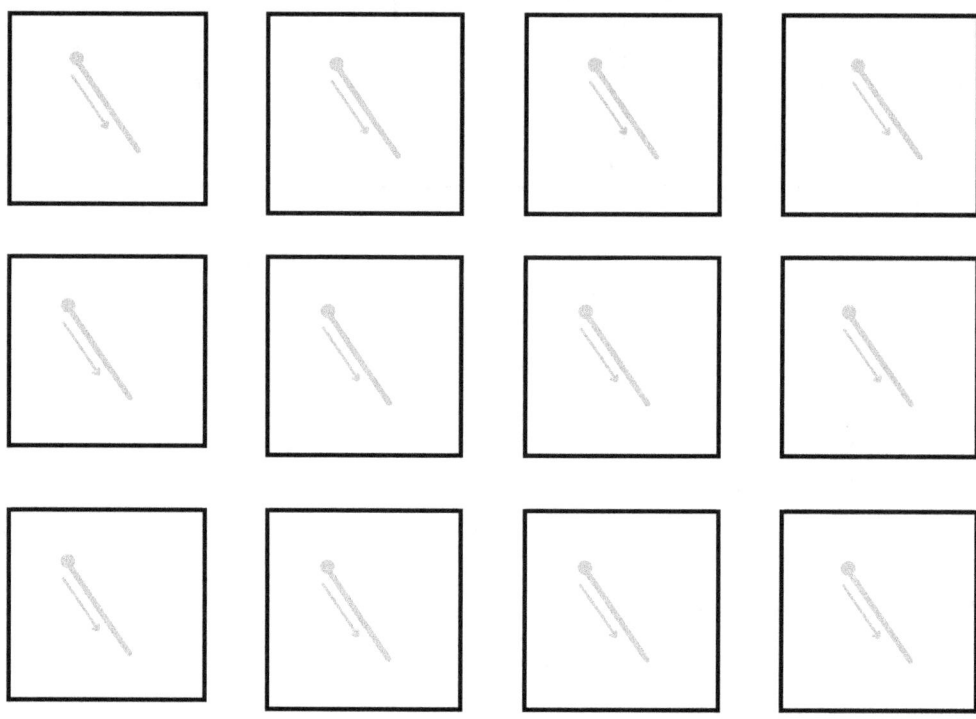

Make a Meteor shower.

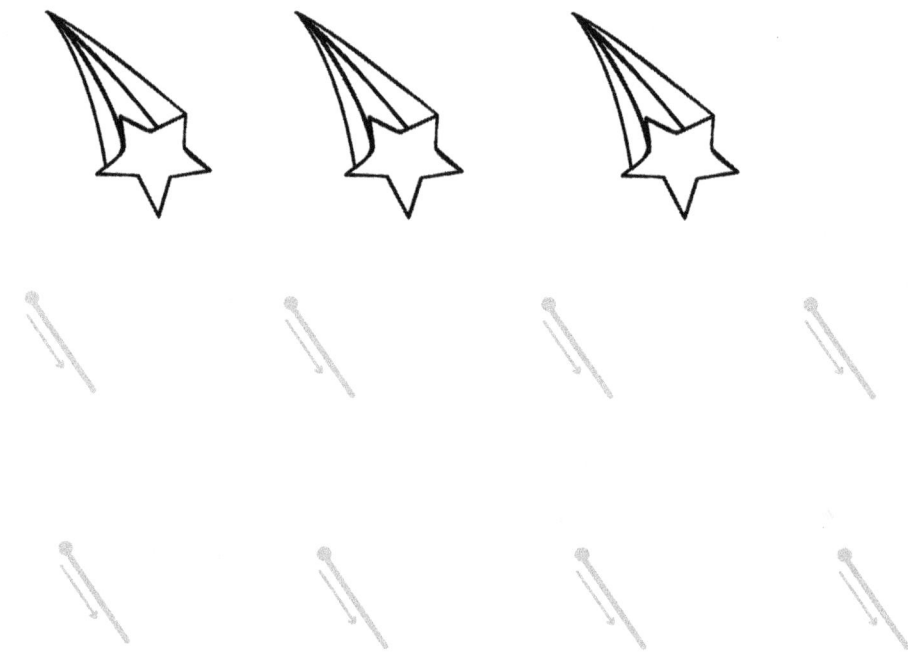

Play ball under the stars.

Draw your own writing patch.

seed   grass   airplane   rain   shooting star

Letter A

Apple

rain   shooting star   airplane

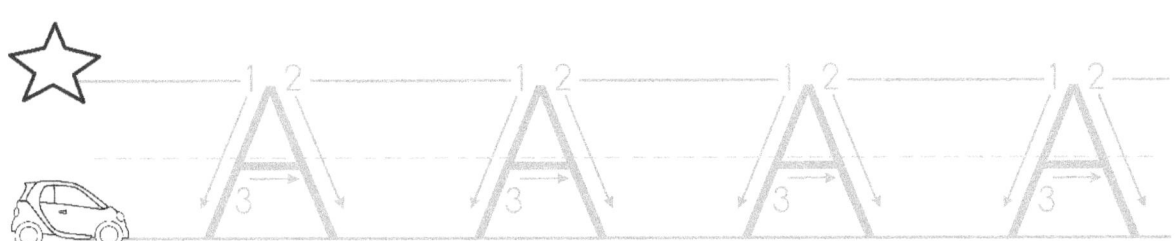

Letter x

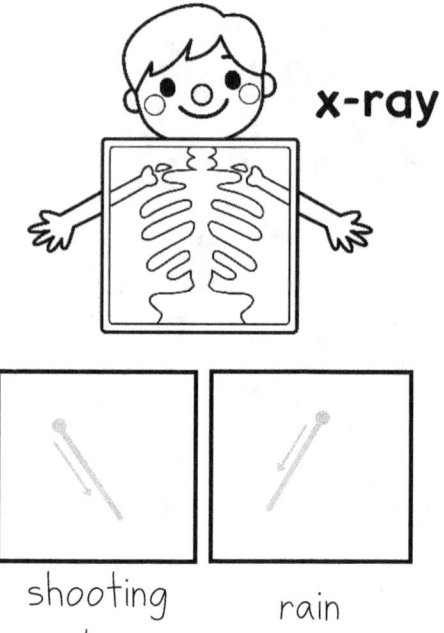

x-ray

shooting star | rain

Letter X

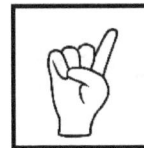  

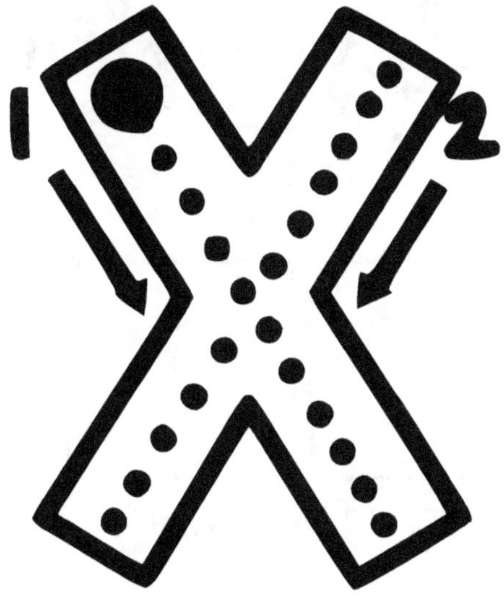

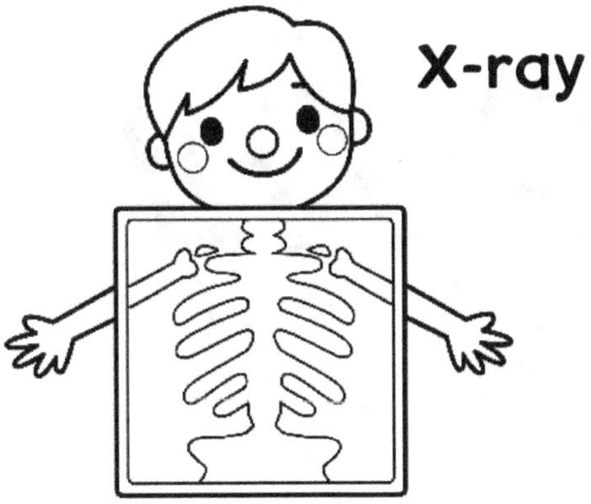

X-ray

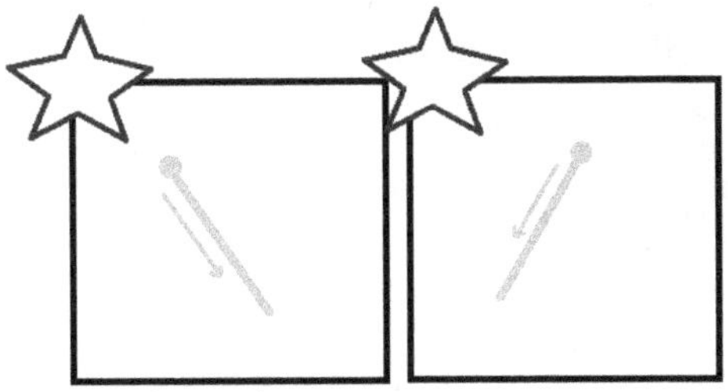

shooting star   rain

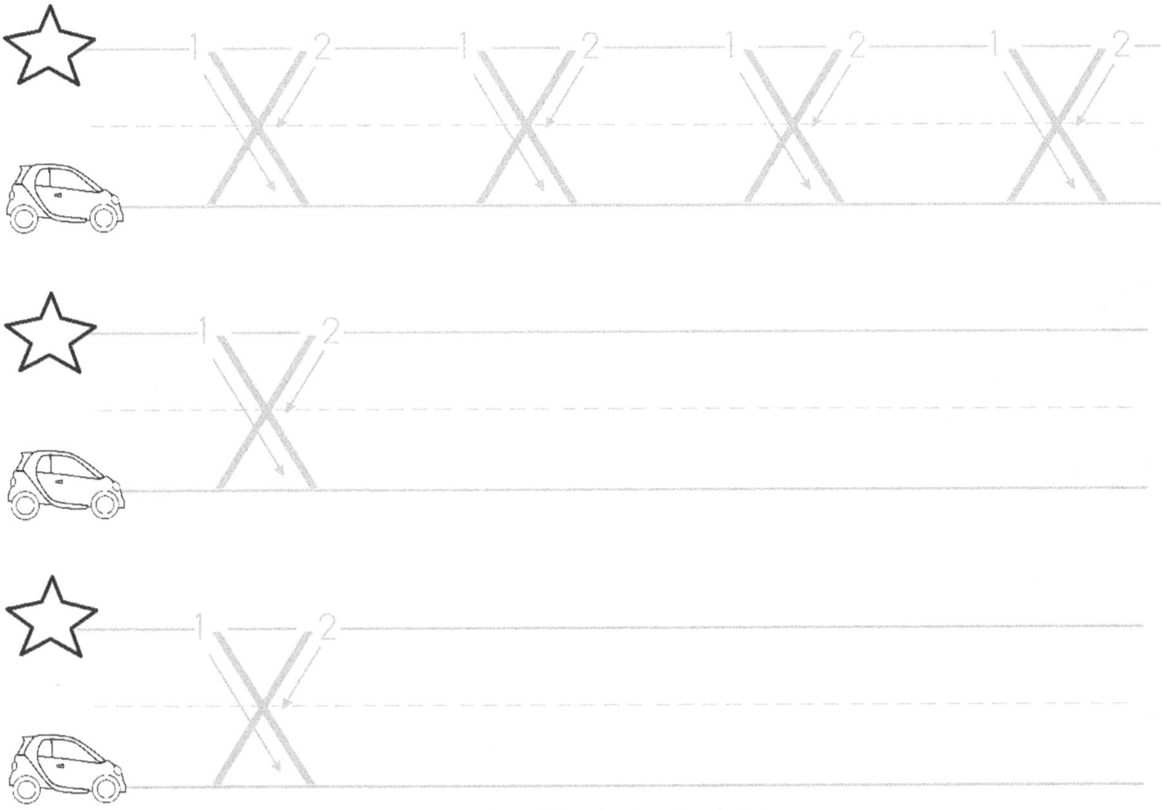

Letter y

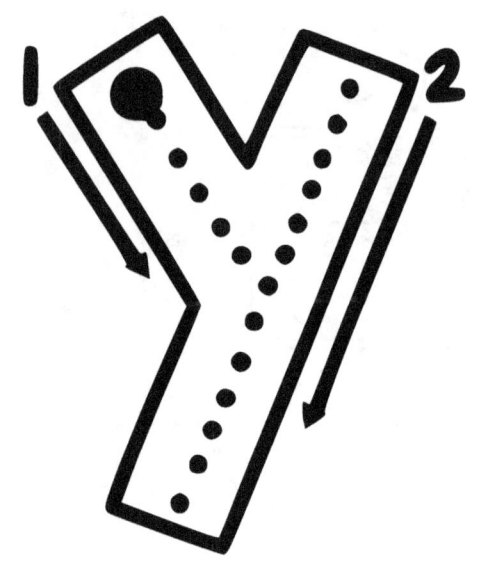

yak

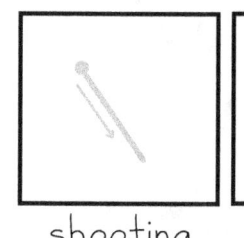 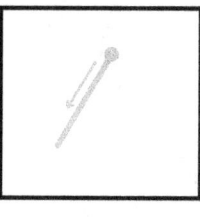

shooting star   rain

Letter Y

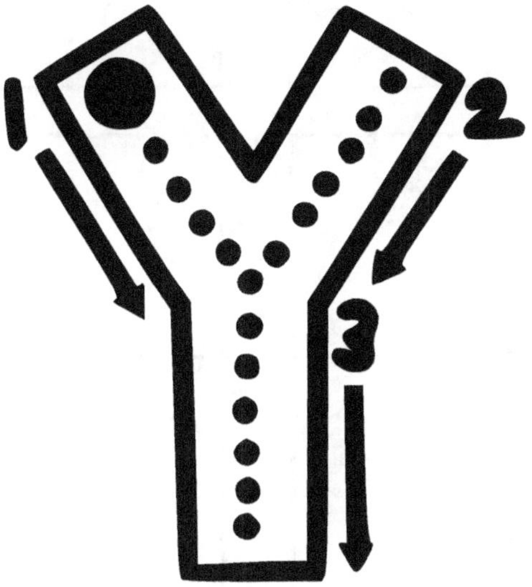

Yak

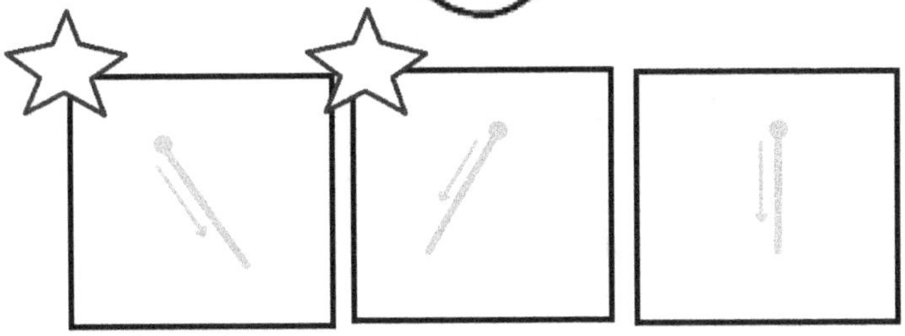

shooting star   rain   grass

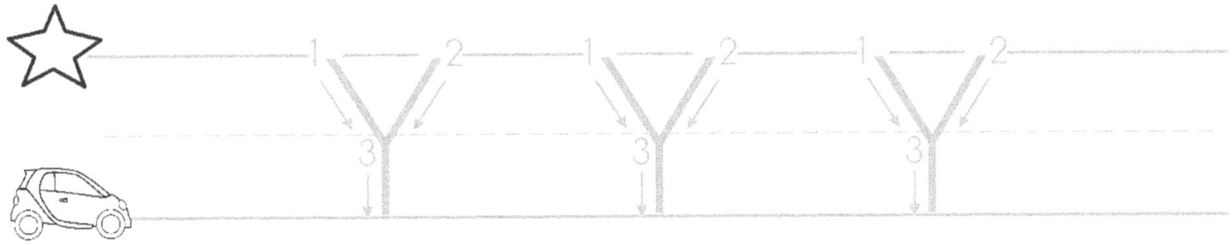

Jump

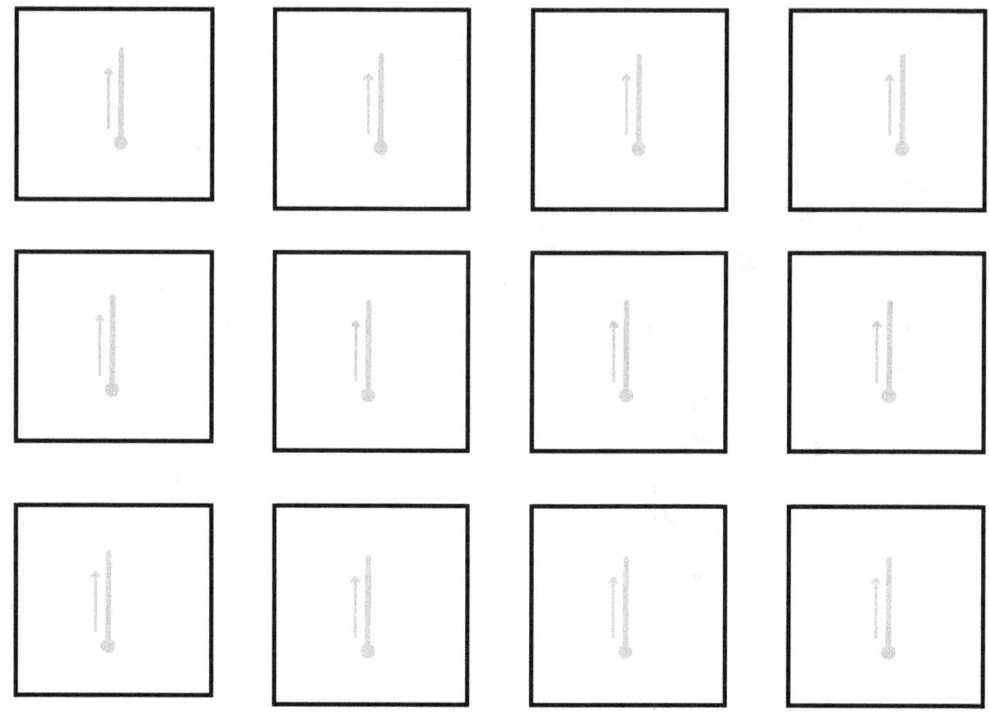

Jump in puddles!

Jump rope.

Draw your own writing patch.

seed   grass   airplane   rain   shooting star   jump

Letter N

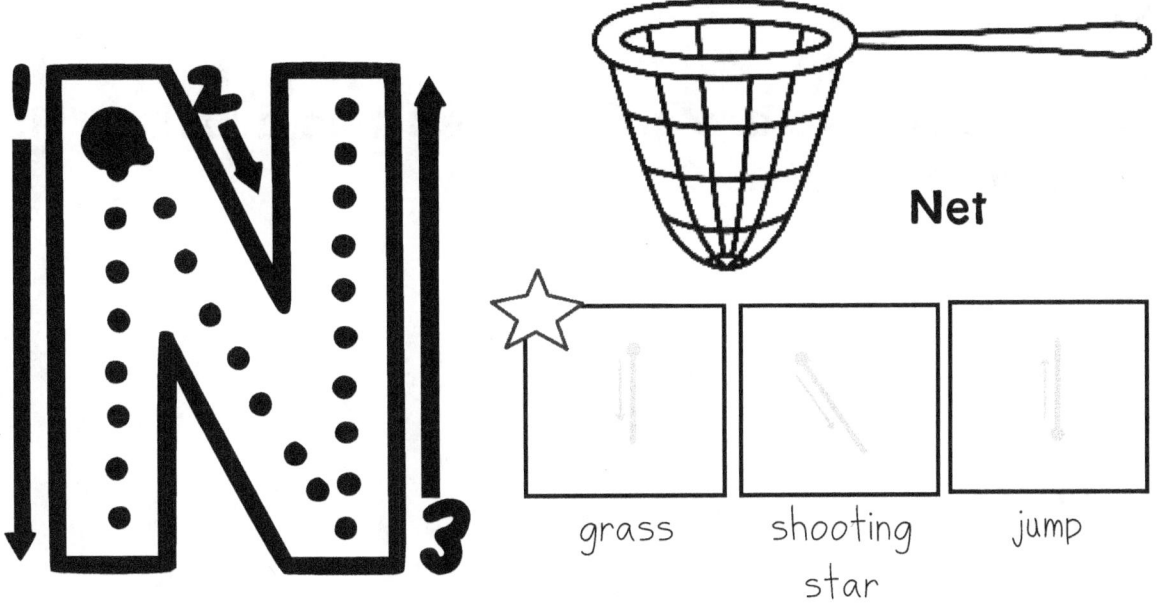

Net

grass   shooting star   jump

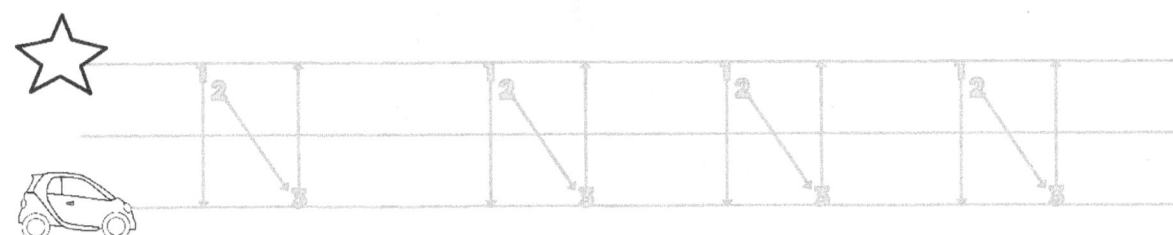

You have done a great job learning all the letters that are made with straight lines! Now we are going to learn how to make curved / rounded strokes in our letters!

The first stroke we are going to learn is a 'ball.' This is what a ball looks like.

ball

The ball swipe looks like this:

You can see that you start at the top of the ball and you swipe to the left, curving down and all the way around.

Teacher Tip!
Repeat and teach frequently...Help students understand this rule... When the letter we are making starts with a ball, we will start at the top of the ball and curve to the left.

Ball

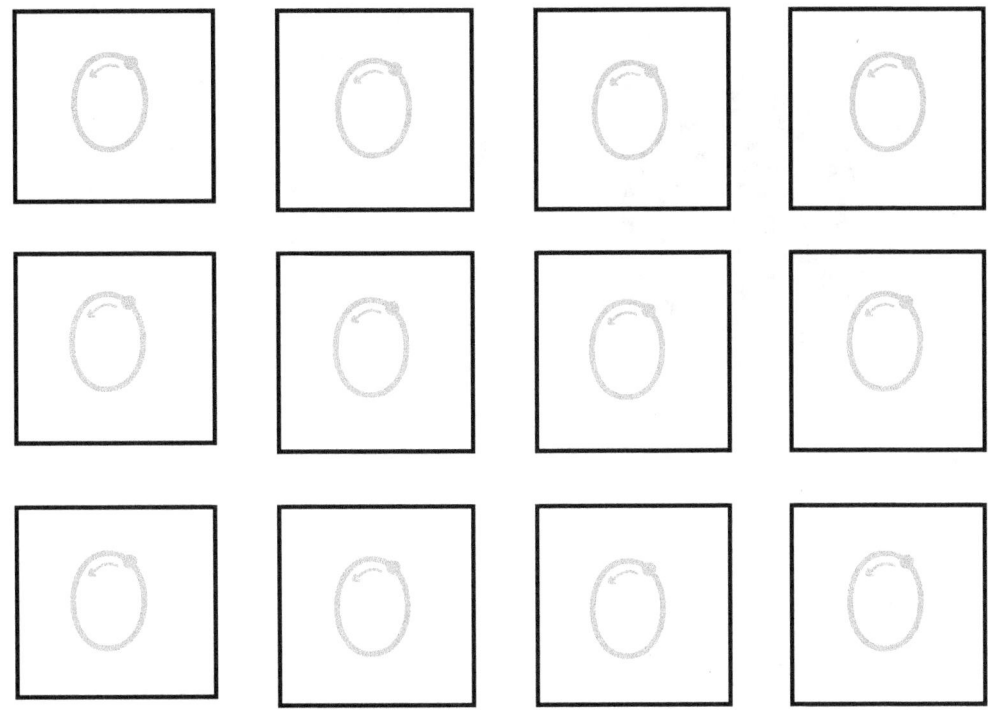

Make a bug in the grass.

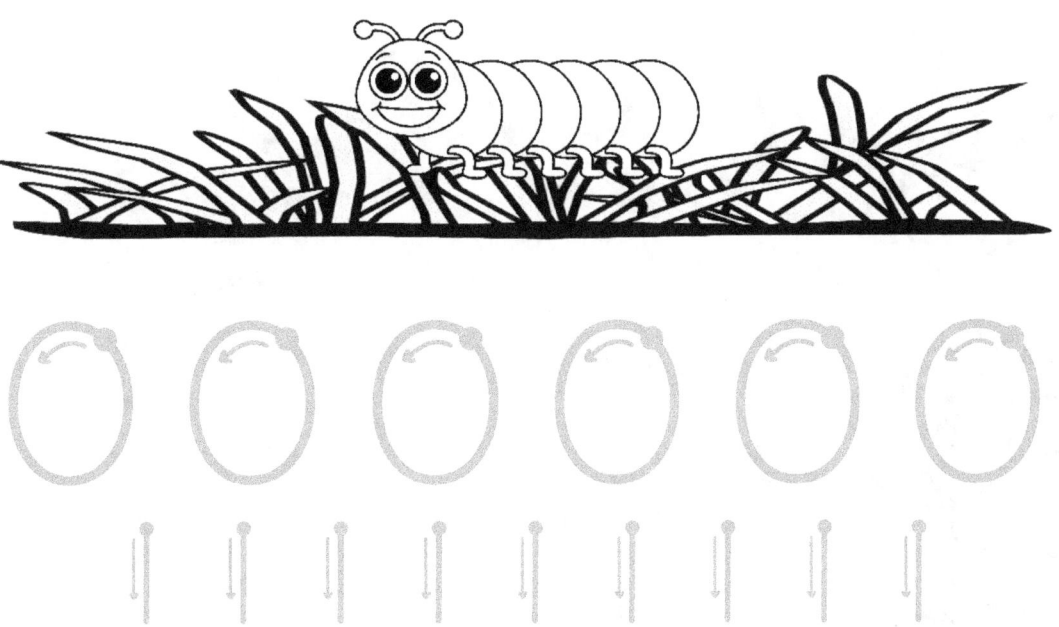

Time to play ball.

Draw your own writing patch.

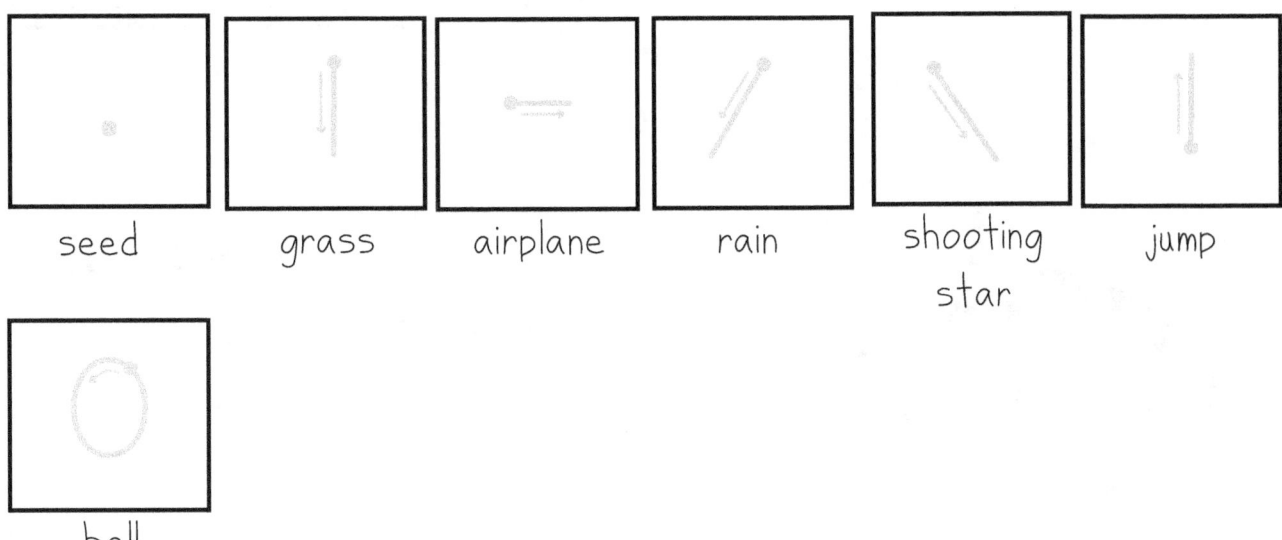

seed   grass   airplane   rain   shooting star   jump

ball

Letter o

octopus

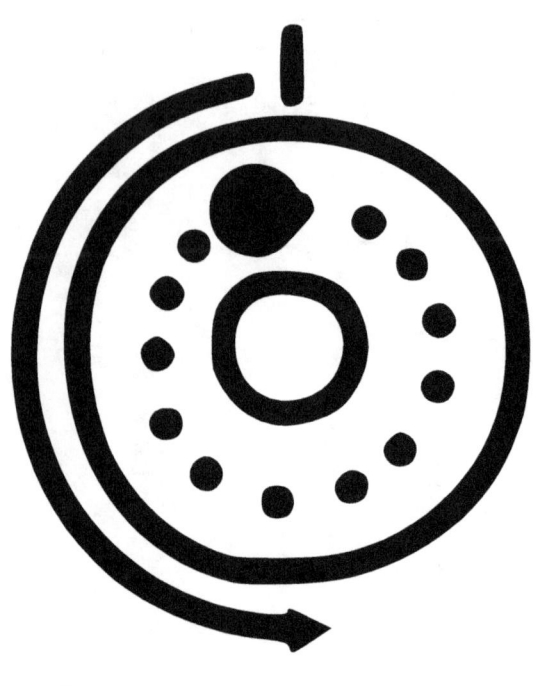

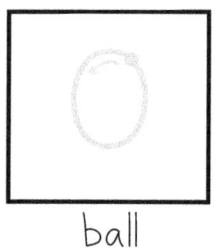
ball

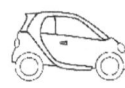

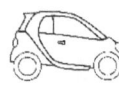

Letter O

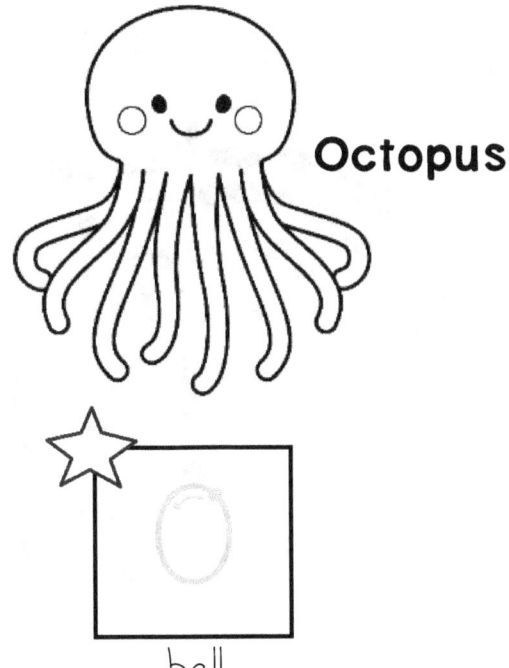

Octopus

ball

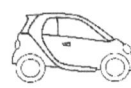

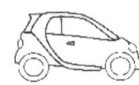

Letter a

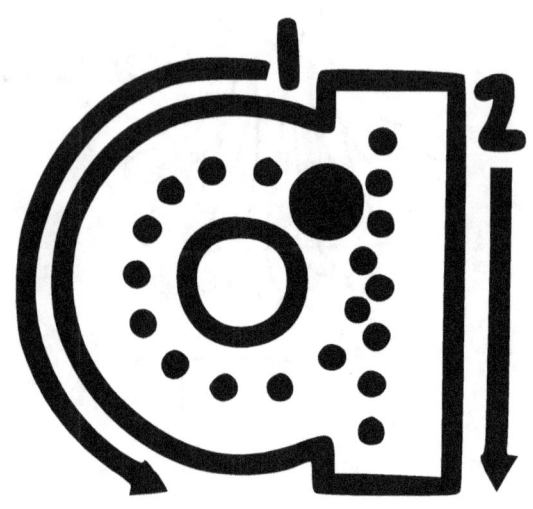

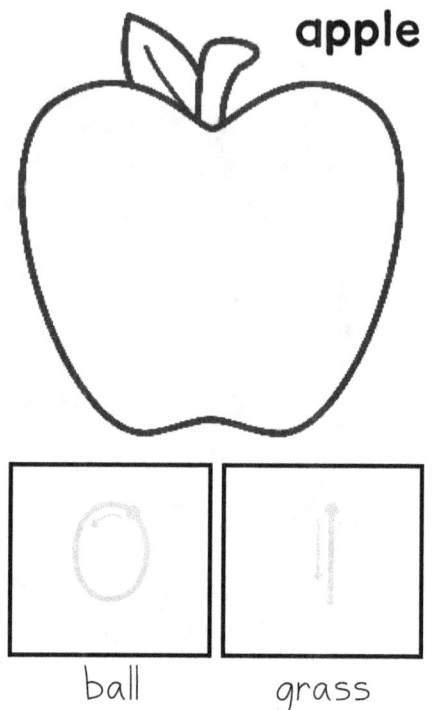

ball   grass

Letter q

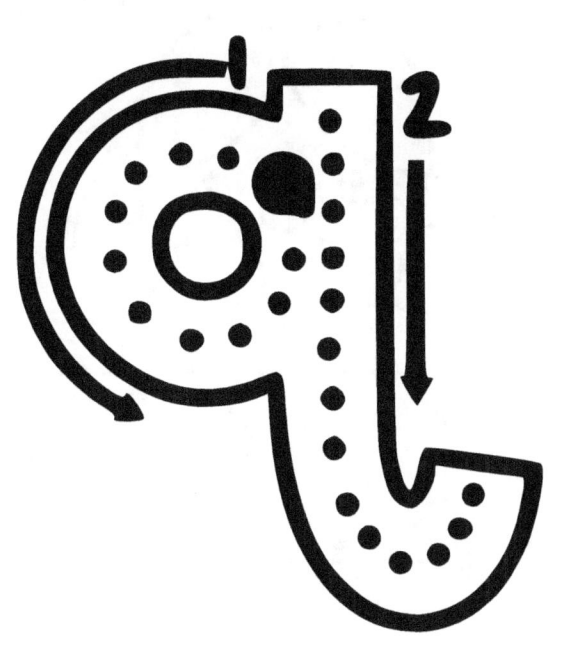

queen

ball   grass

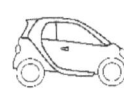

Letter Q

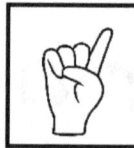  

Queen

ball | shooting star

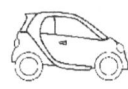

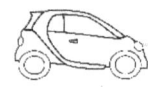

Sun

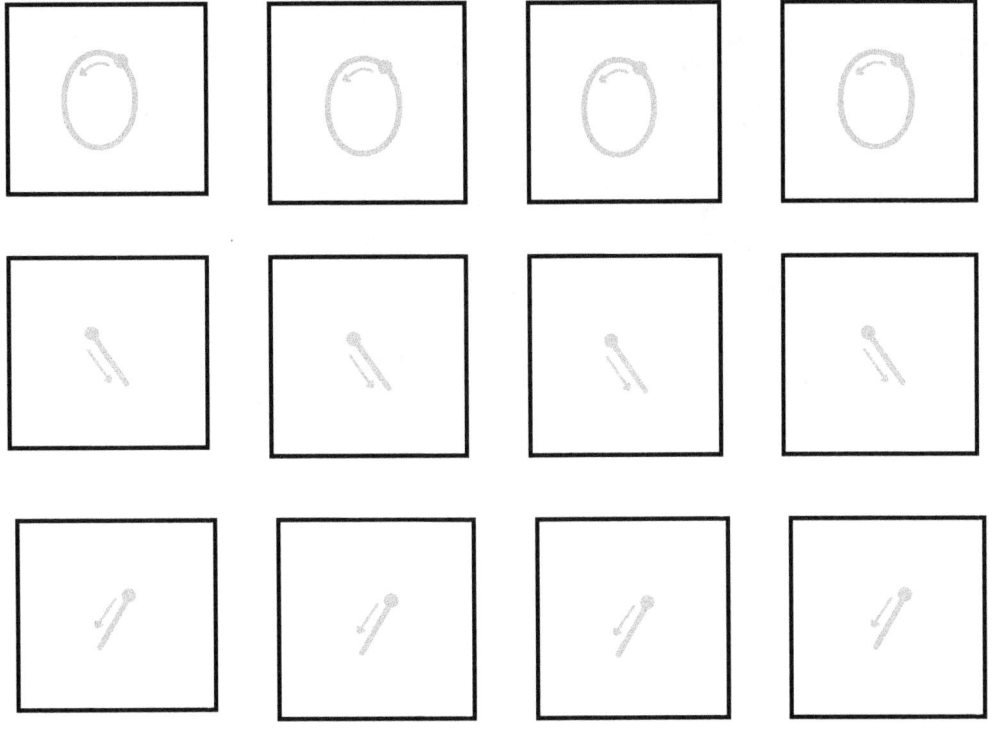

Make a sun.

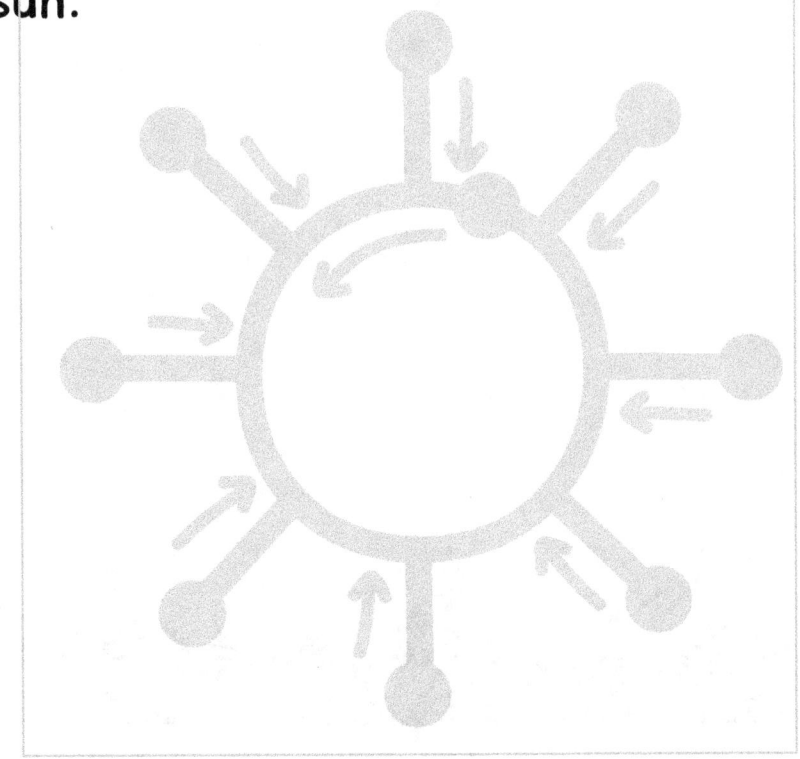

Make a sun with an airplane and grass.

Make a sun with a bug and rain.

Make a moon with shooting stars.

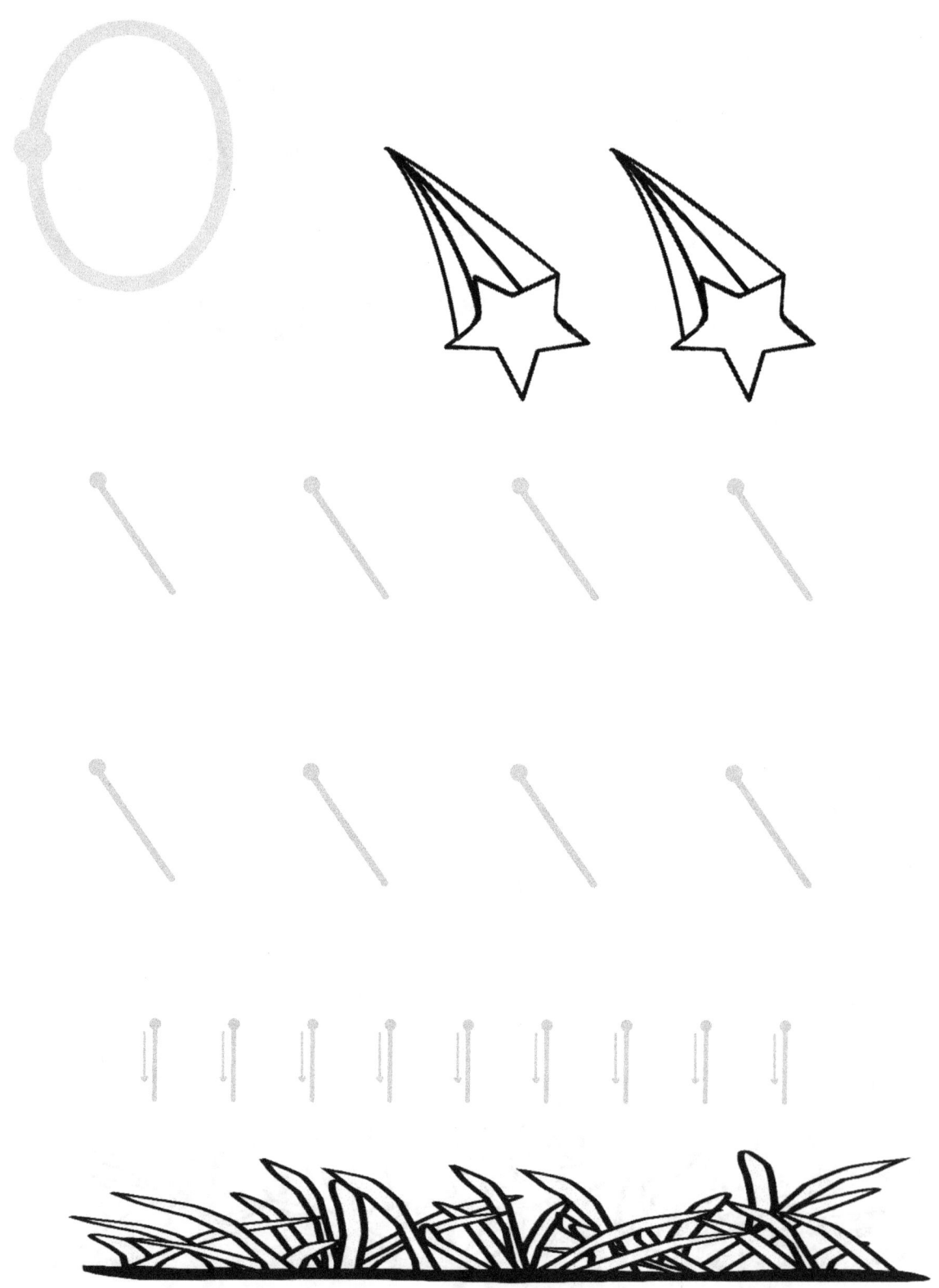

Draw your own writing patch.

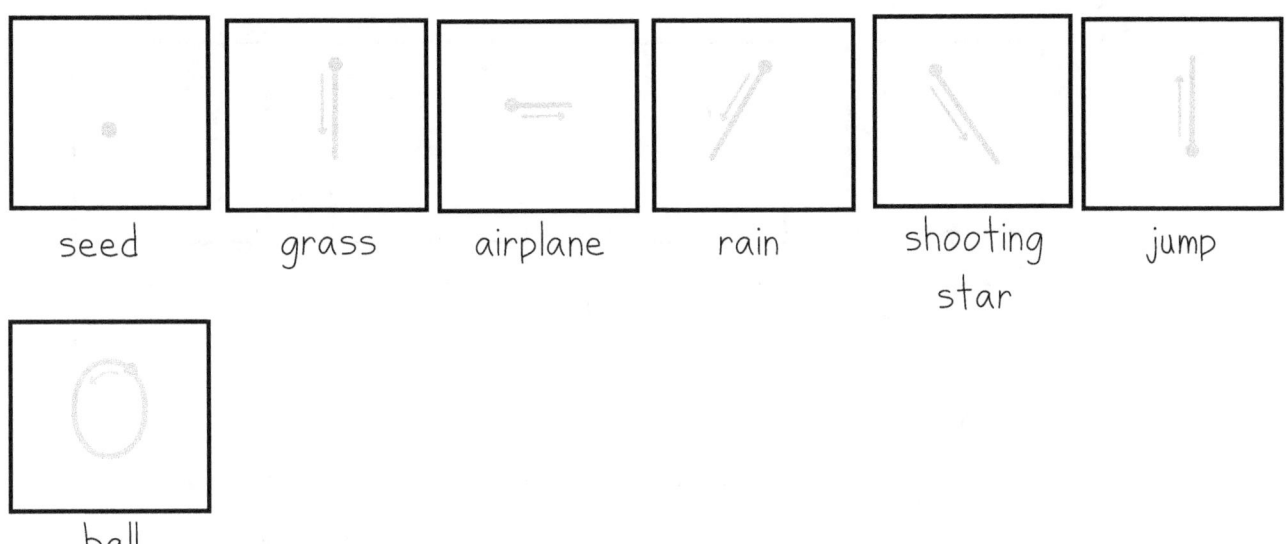

seed   grass   airplane   rain   shooting star   jump

ball

Rainbow

Make a rainbow.

Look at the rainbow.

Draw your own writing patch.

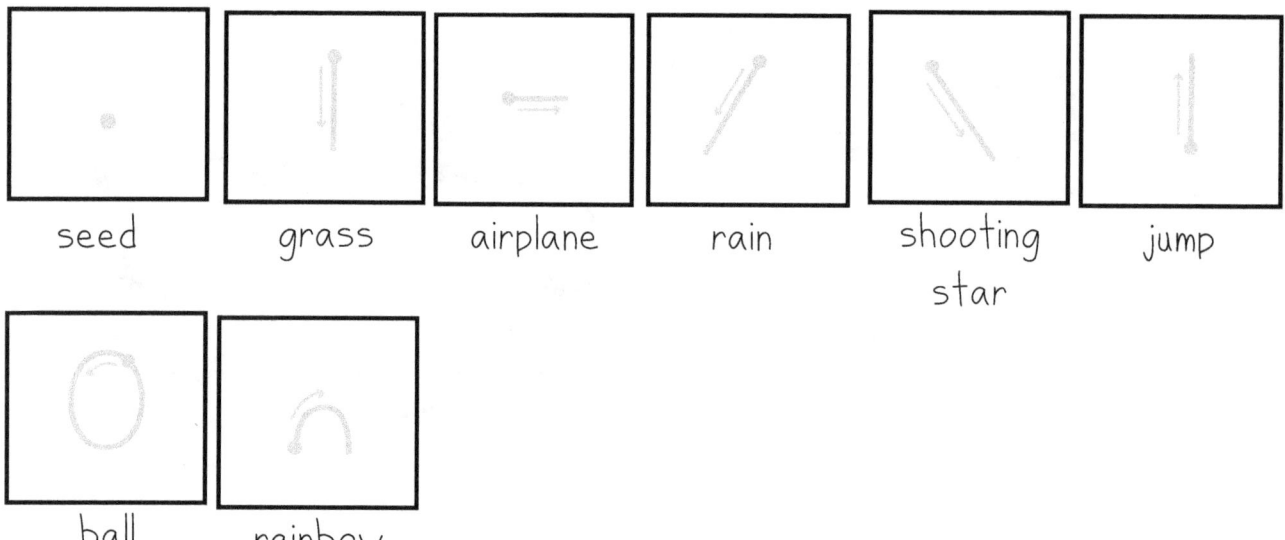

seed   grass   airplane   rain   shooting star   jump

ball   rainbow

Letter n

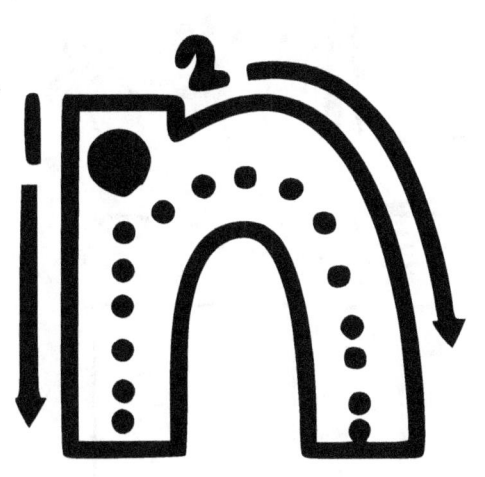

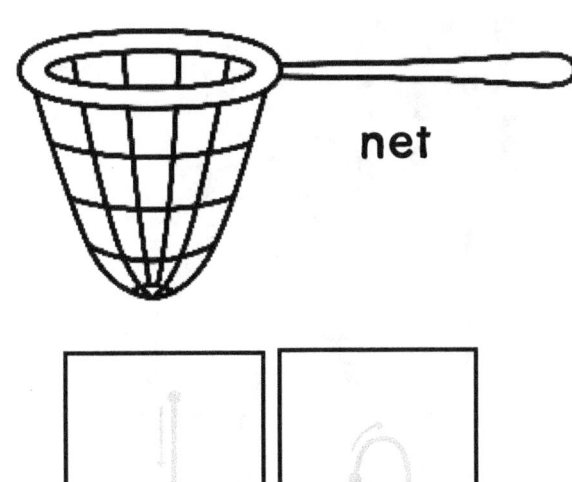

net

grass   rainbow

Letter h

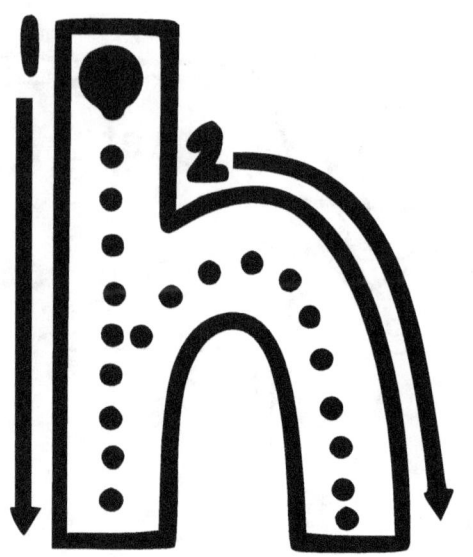

helicopter

grass   rainbow

Letter m

mouse

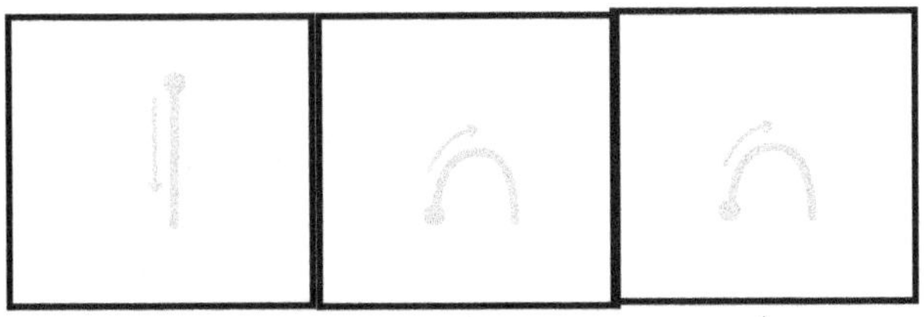

grass rainbow rainbow

Smile

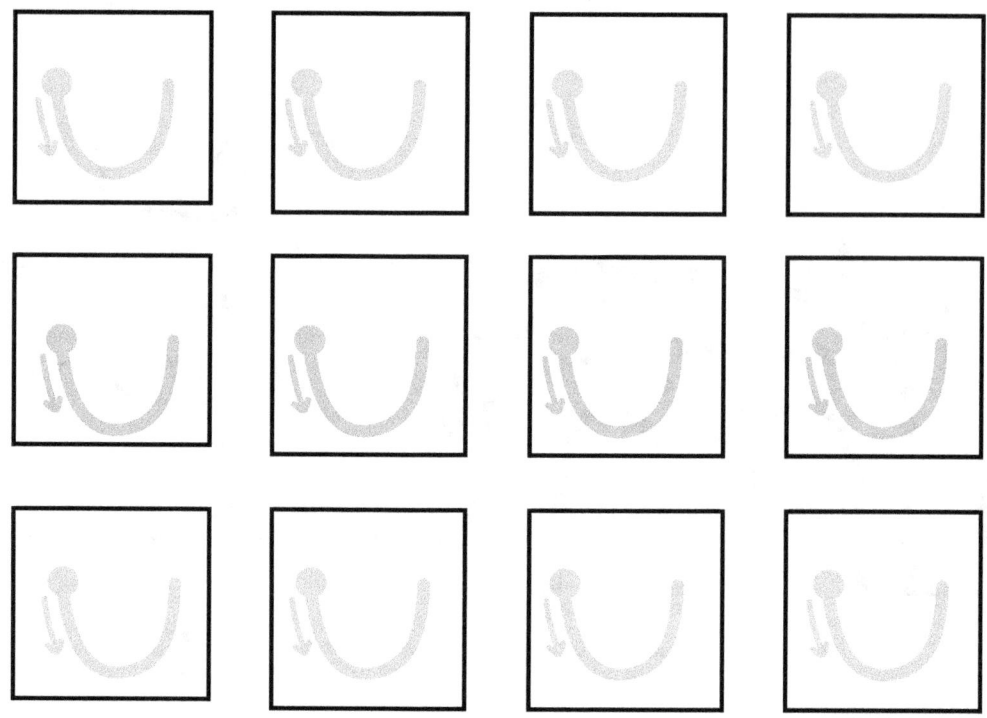

Make a smile.

Say cheese and smile for the camera!

Draw your own writing patch.

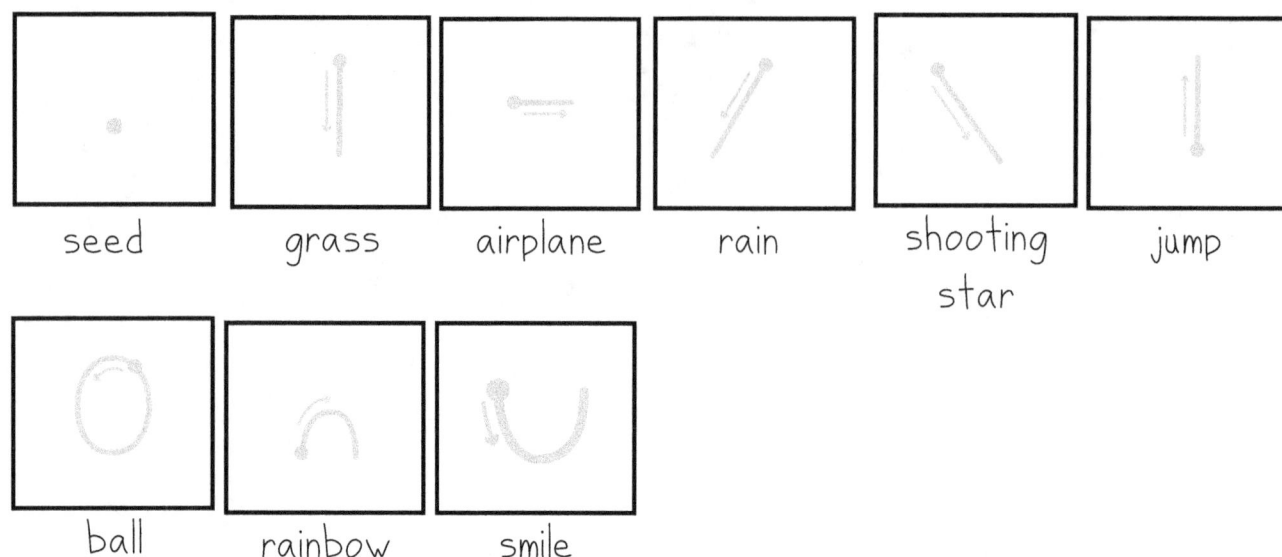

Letter U

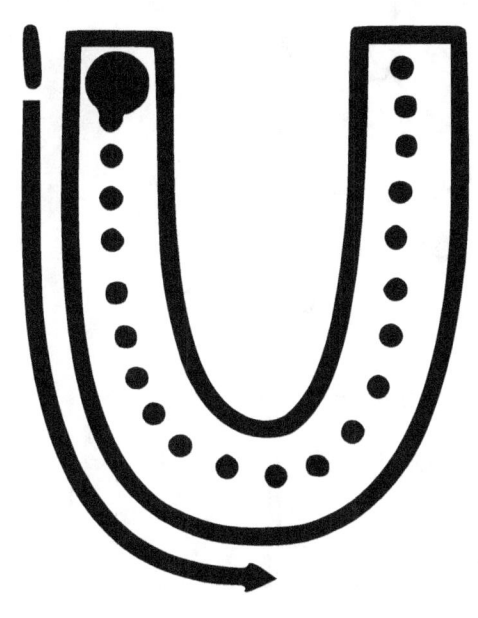

unicorn

smile

Letter u

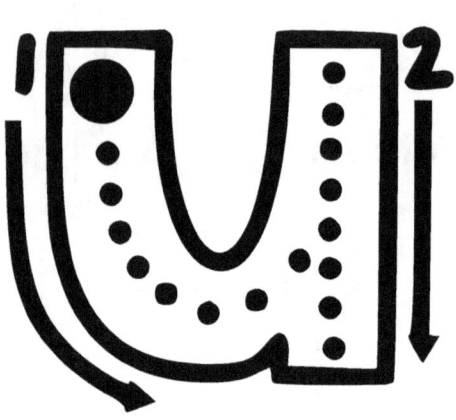

unicorn

smile   grass

Make a bunny in the grass.

Make a bunny in the sun.

Make a rainbow in the sun and rain.

Ears

Make a smile with ears.

Make a flower!

Make a flower!

Draw your own writing patch.

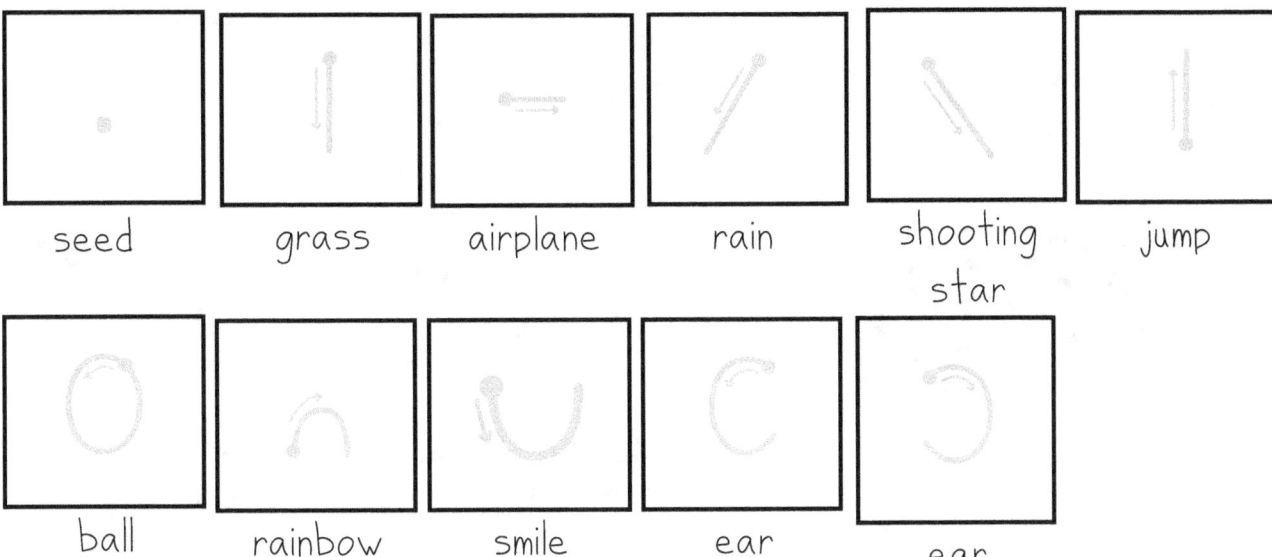

| seed | grass | airplane | rain | shooting star | jump |

| ball | rainbow | smile | ear | ear |

Letter c

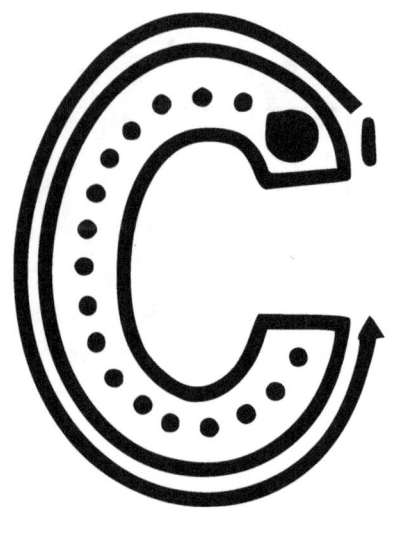

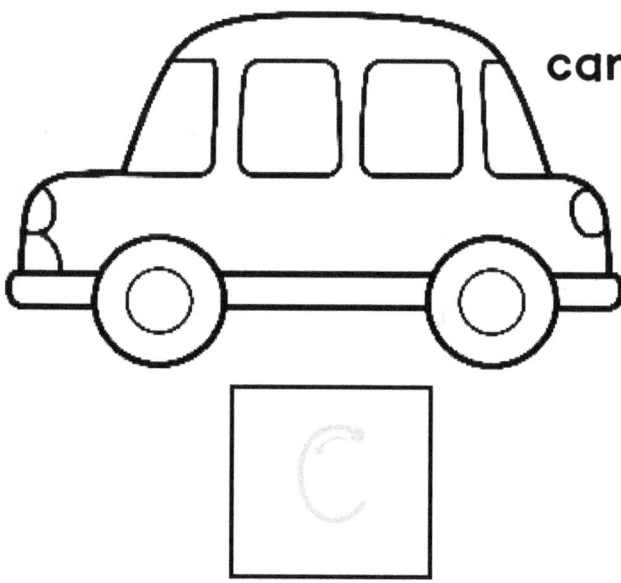

car

ear

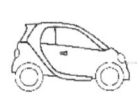

Letter C

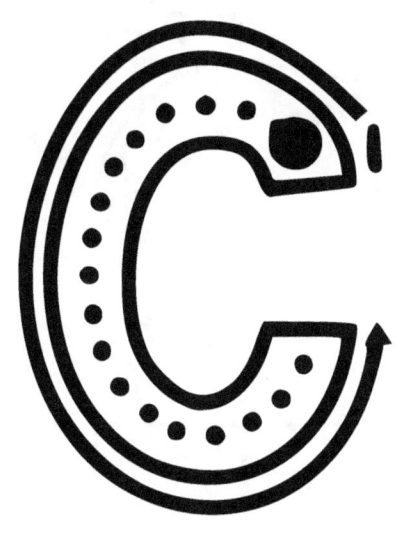

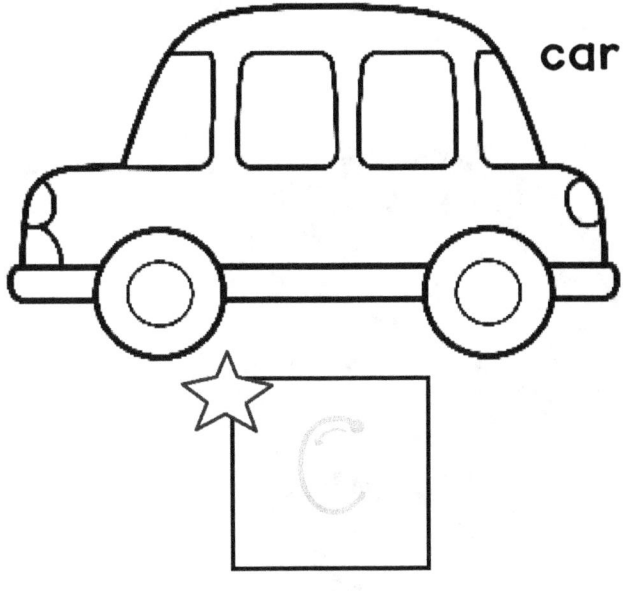

car

ear

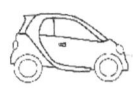

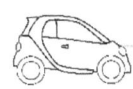

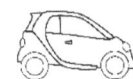

Letter e

elephant

airplane   ear

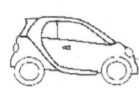 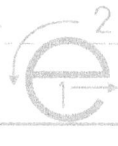

Letter G

Letter d

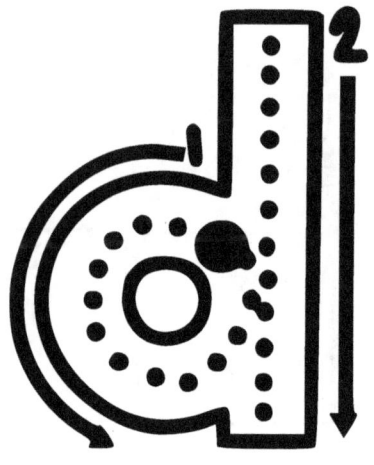

dinosaur

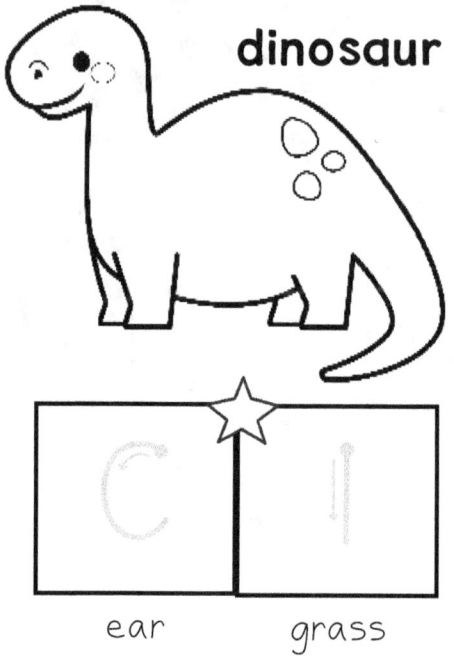

ear   grass

Letter D

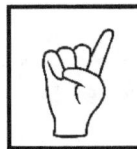  

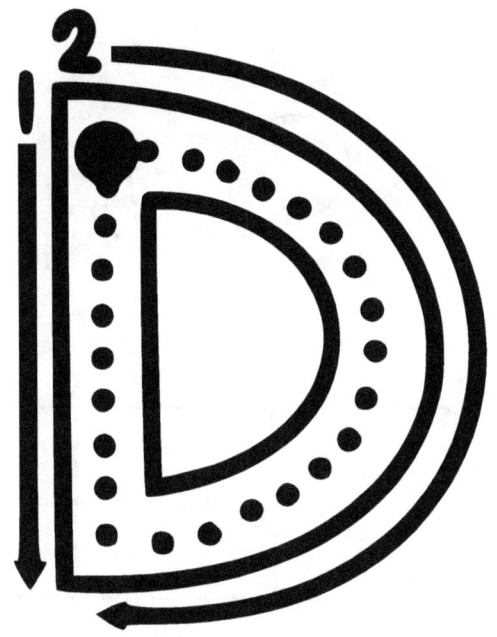

dinosaur

grass   ear

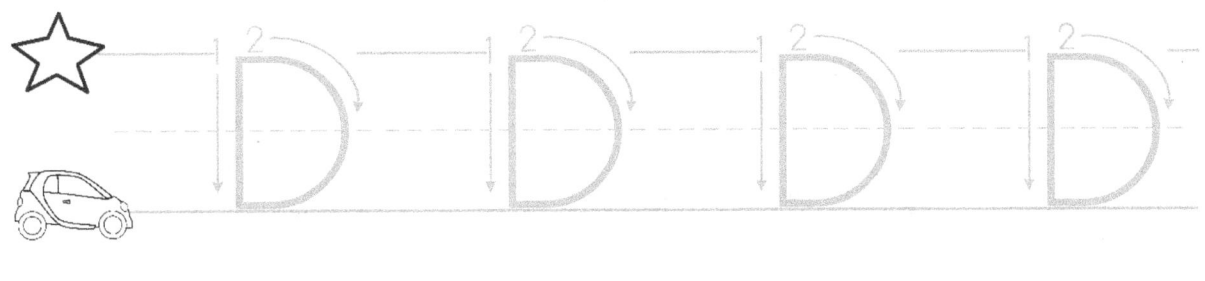

Letter b

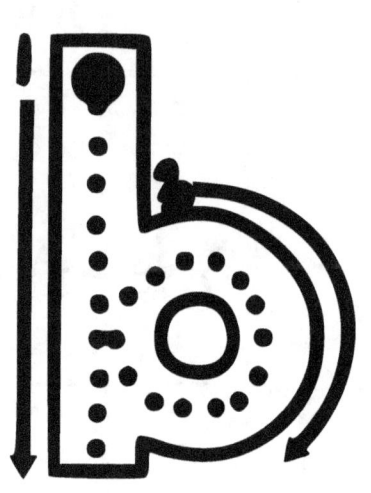

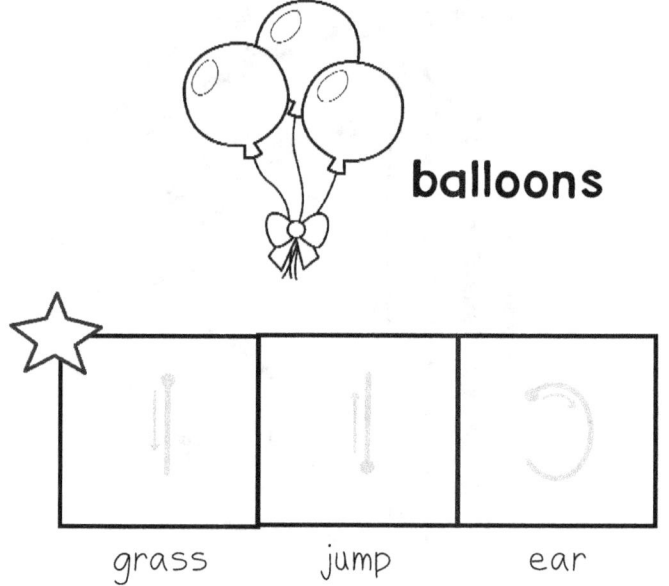

balloons

grass   jump   ear

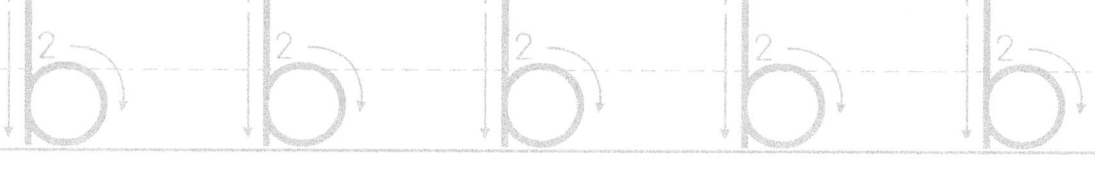

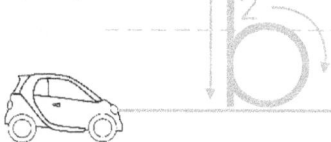

Letter B

Balloons

grass   ear   ear

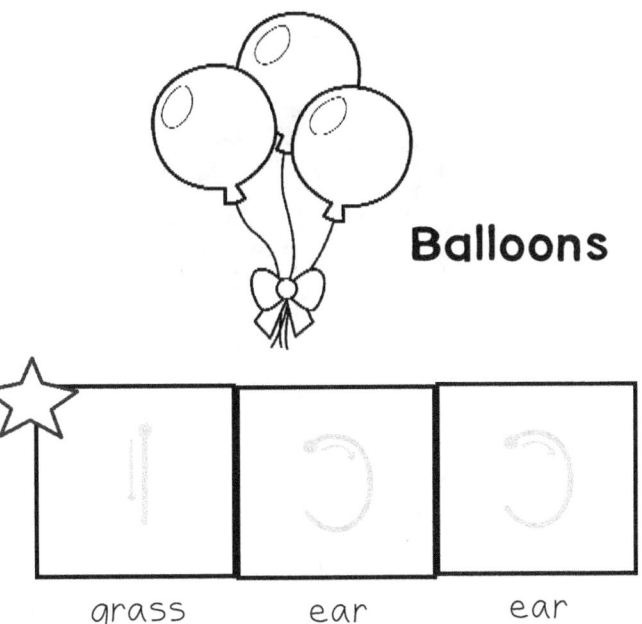

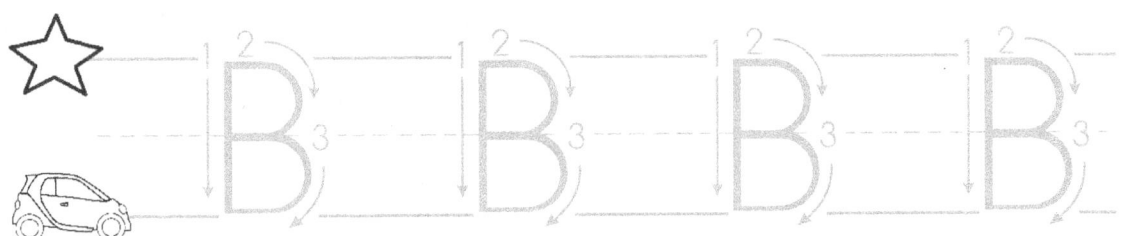

Letter p

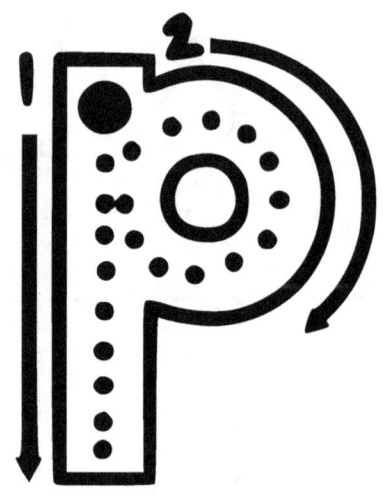 

pig

grass   ear

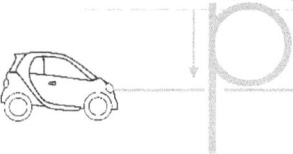   

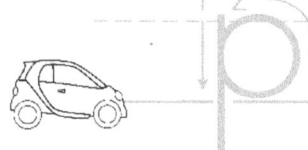

Letter P

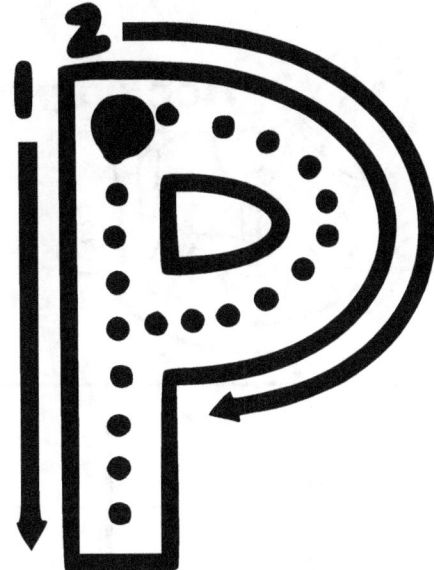

pig

grass ear

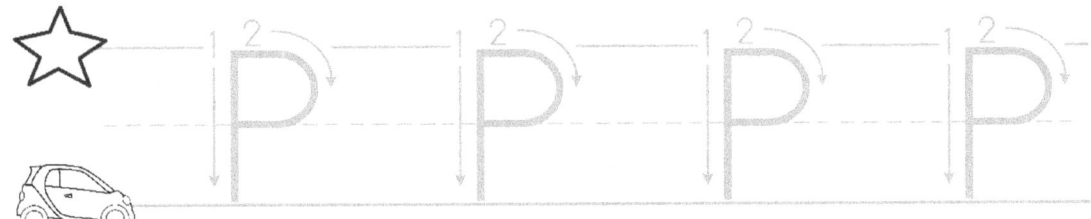

Letter R

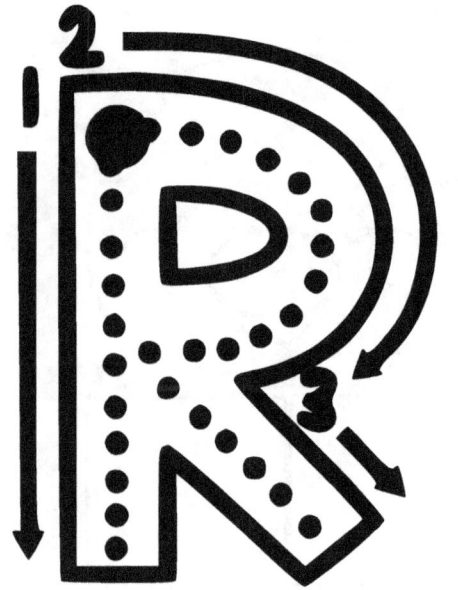

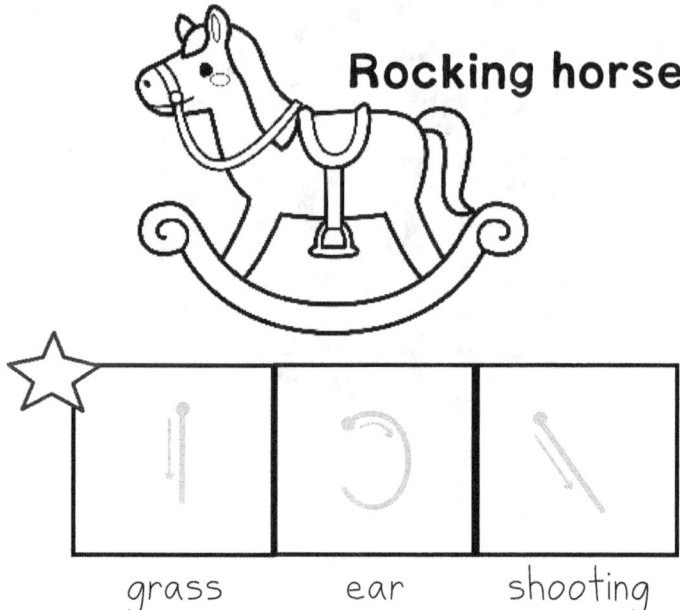

Rocking horse

grass   ear   shooting star

Letter R

Make a sun and flower in the grass and rain.

Bird

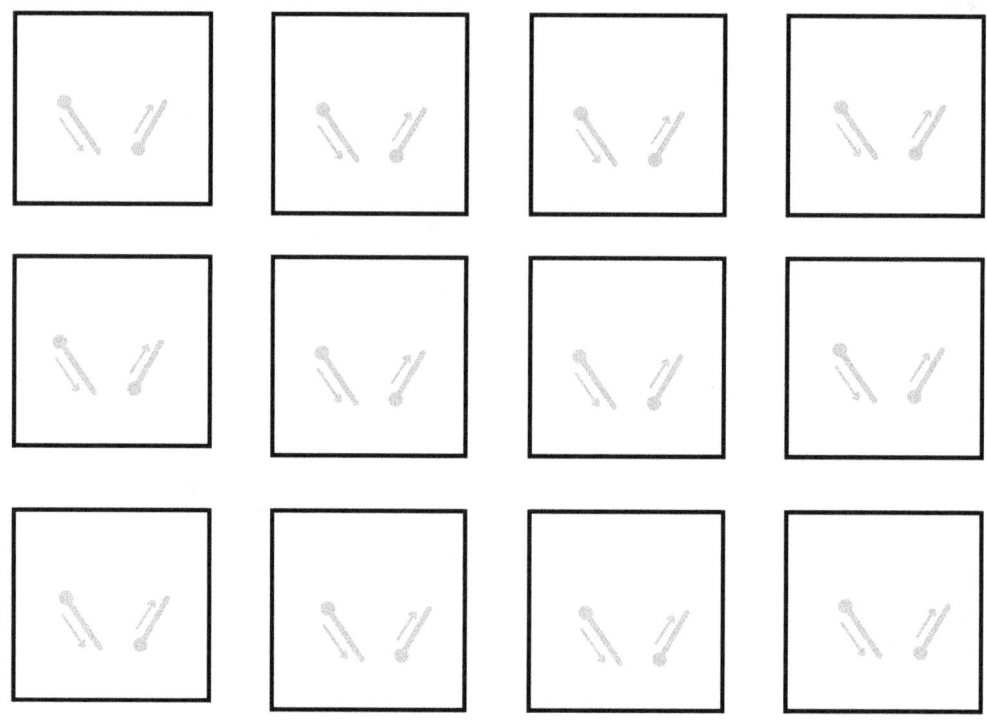

Make birds in the sky.

Birds fly over the rainbow.

The birds like the flower.

Draw your own writing patch.

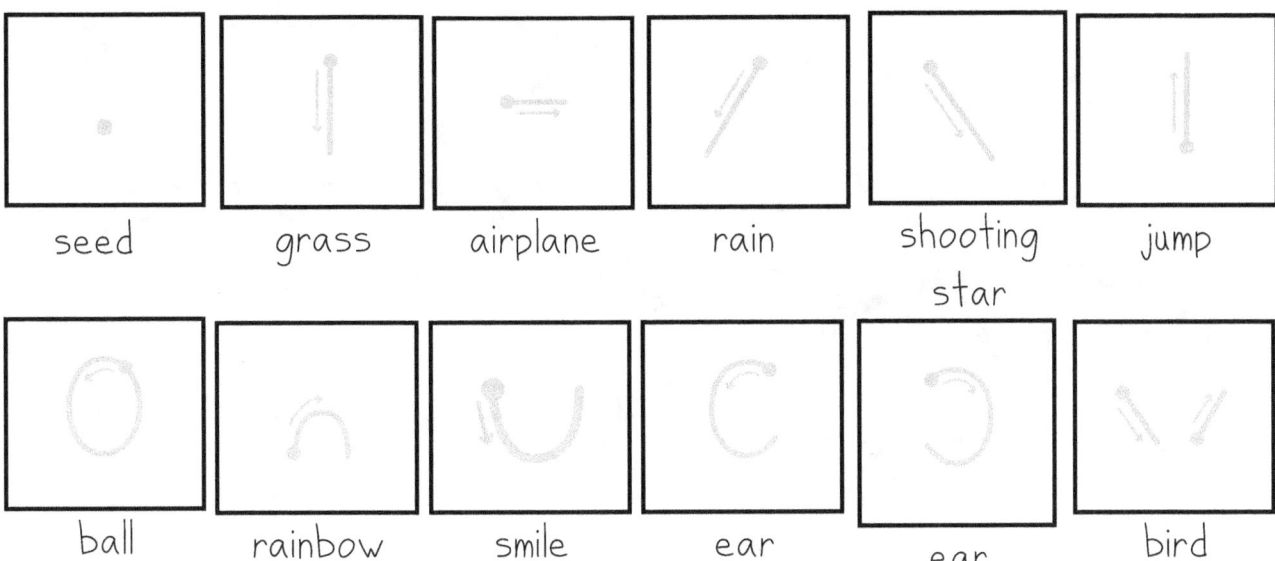

| seed | grass | airplane | rain | shooting star | jump |

| ball | rainbow | smile | ear | ear | bird |

Letter v

van

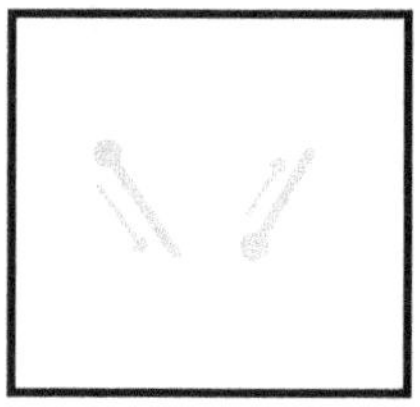

bird

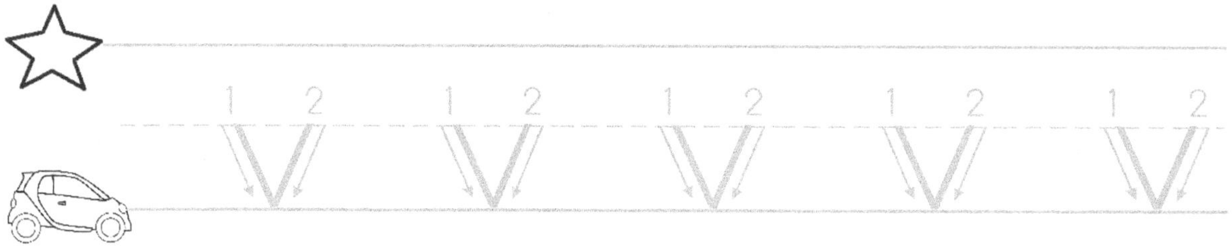

Letter V

van

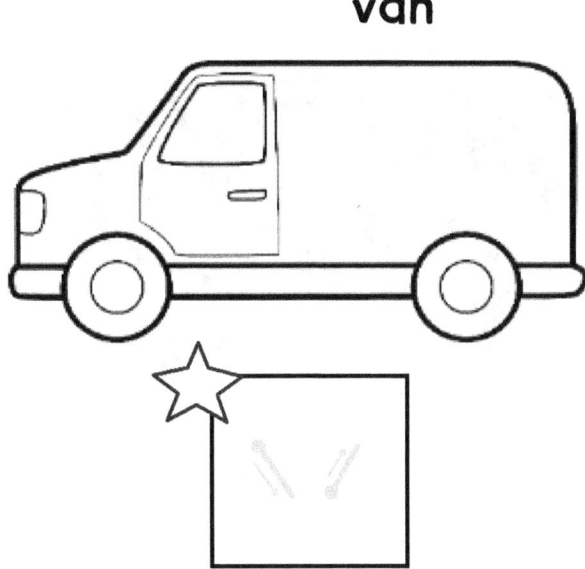

bird

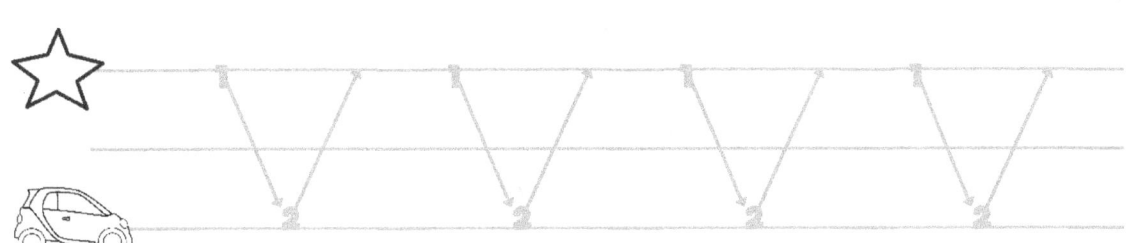

Letter w

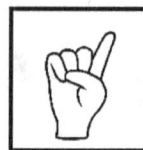  

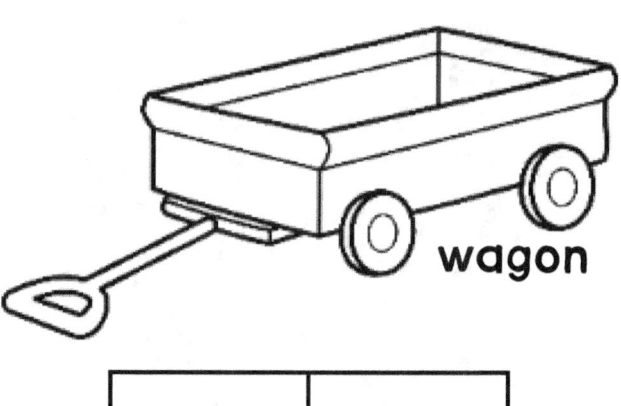

wagon

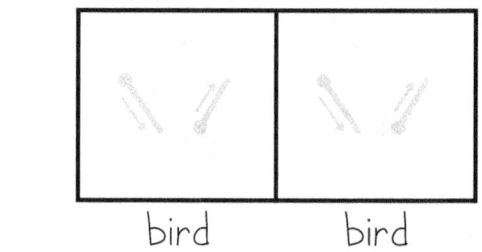

bird   bird

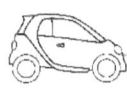

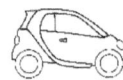

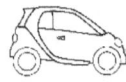

©2019 HandwritingPatch.com

Letter w

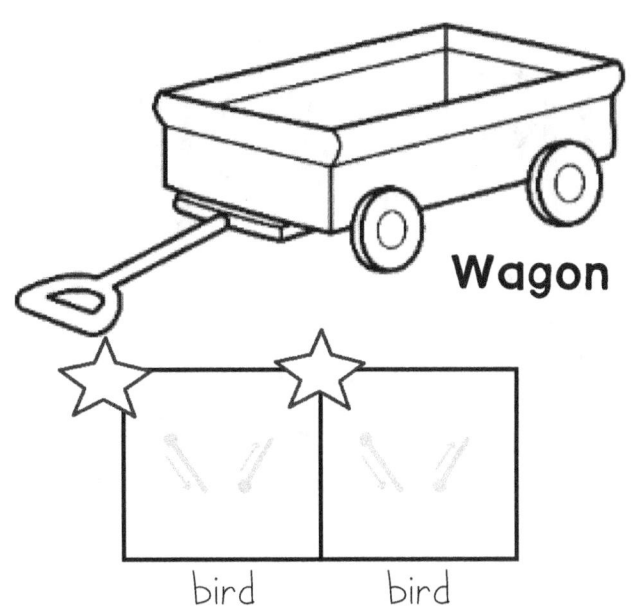

Wagon

bird   bird

 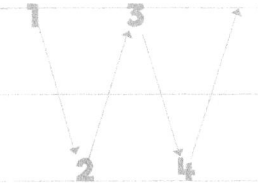 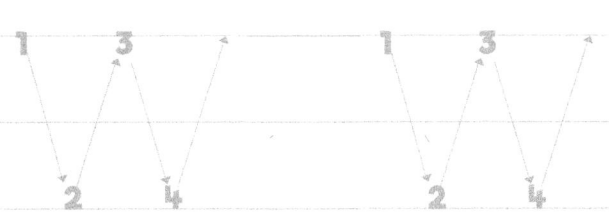

 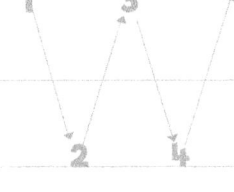

Letter M

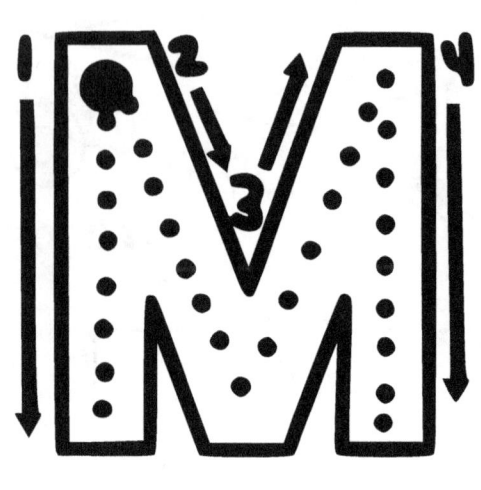

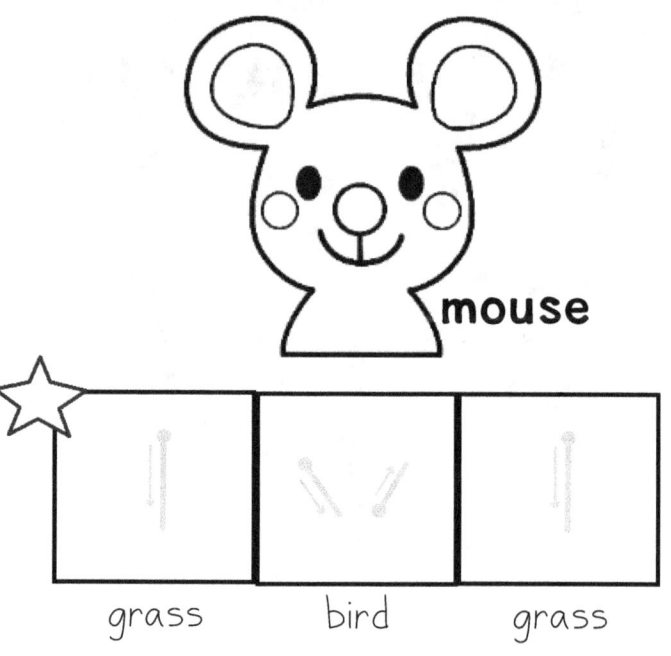

| grass | bird | grass |

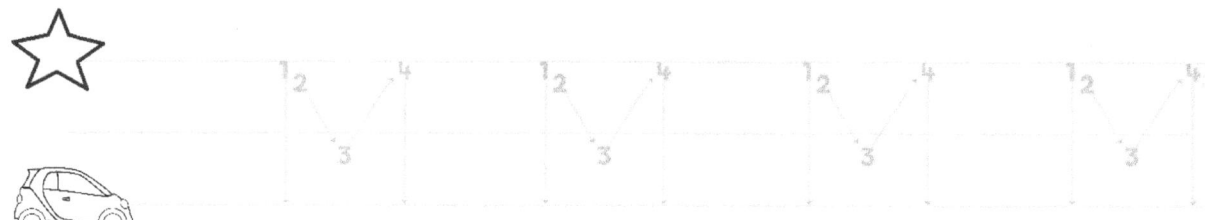

Alligator

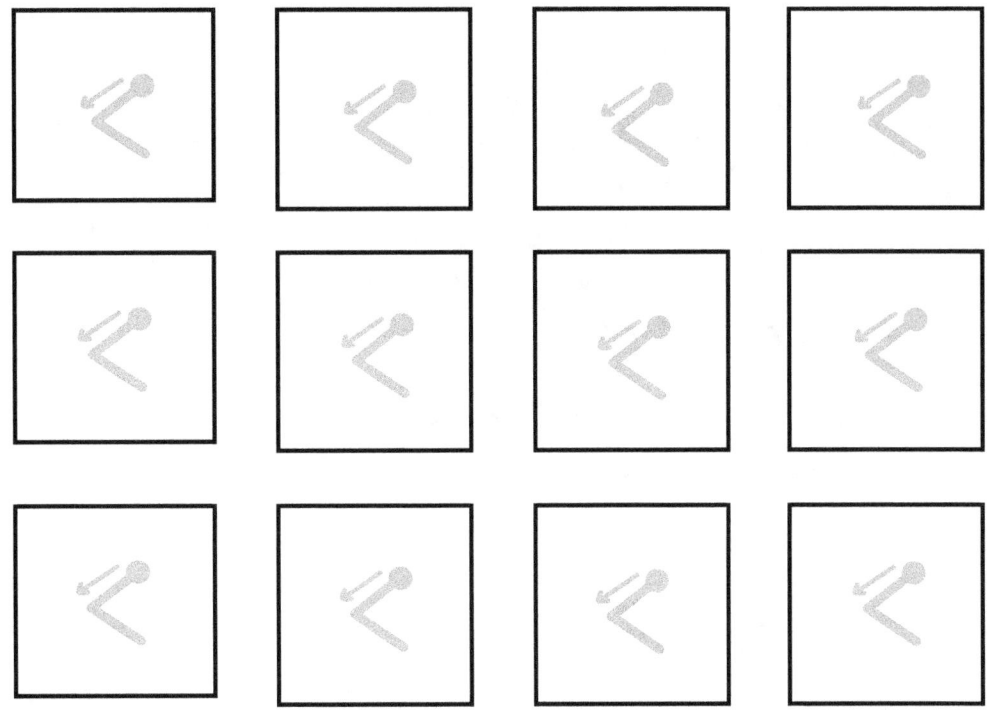

Make alligators.

Look out for the alligator!

Draw your own writing patch.

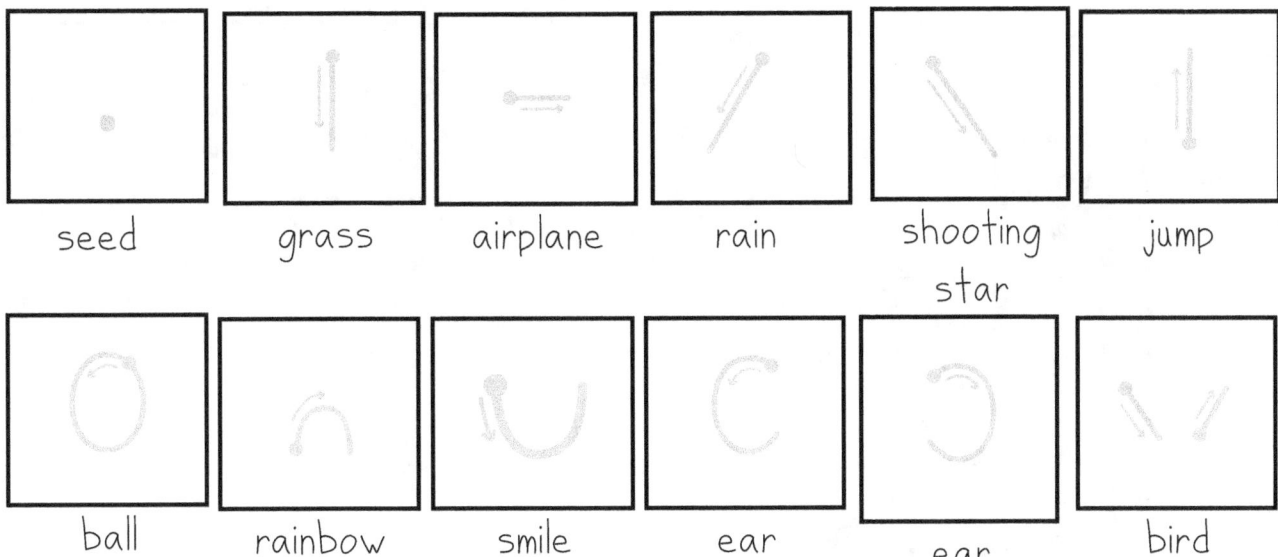

| seed | grass | airplane | rain | shooting star | jump |

| ball | rainbow | smile | ear | ear | bird |

alligator

Letter k

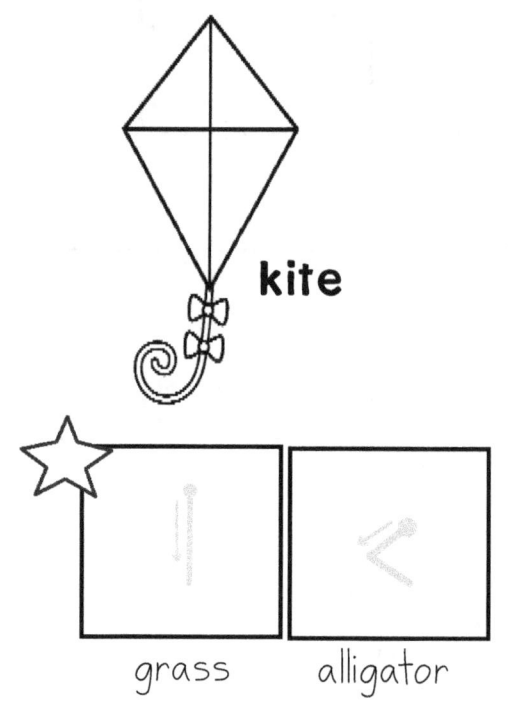

kite

grass   alligator

Letter K

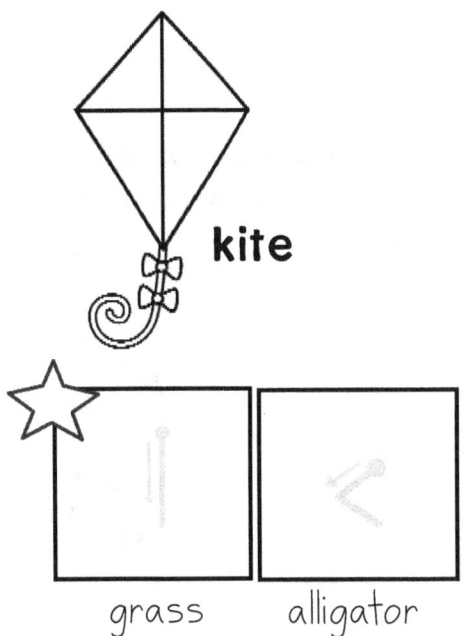

kite

grass   alligator

Letter z

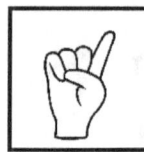  

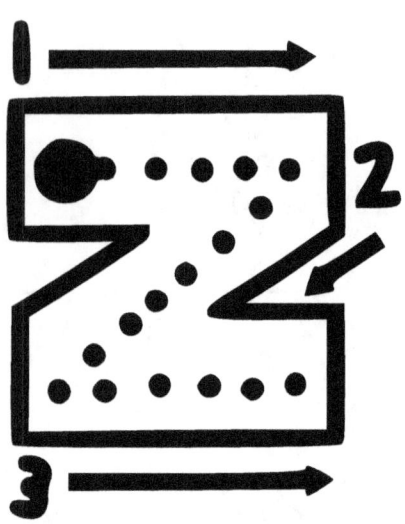

zebra

airplane alligator

Letter z

airplane   alligator

Candy Cane

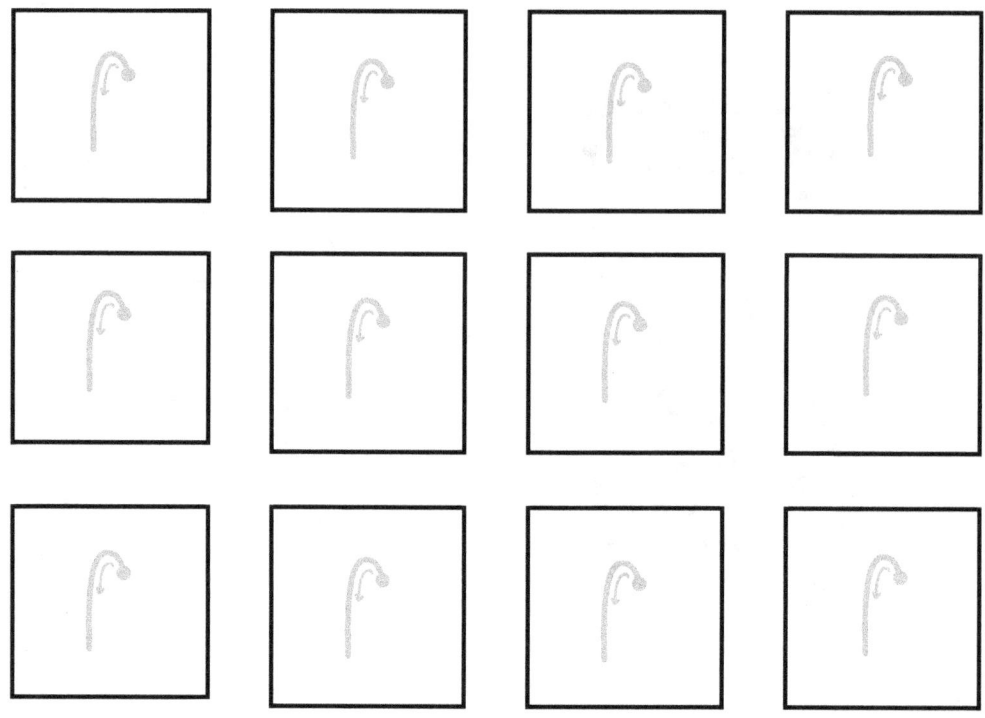

Make a Candy Cane land!

Time for a treat!

Draw your own writing patch.

Letter f

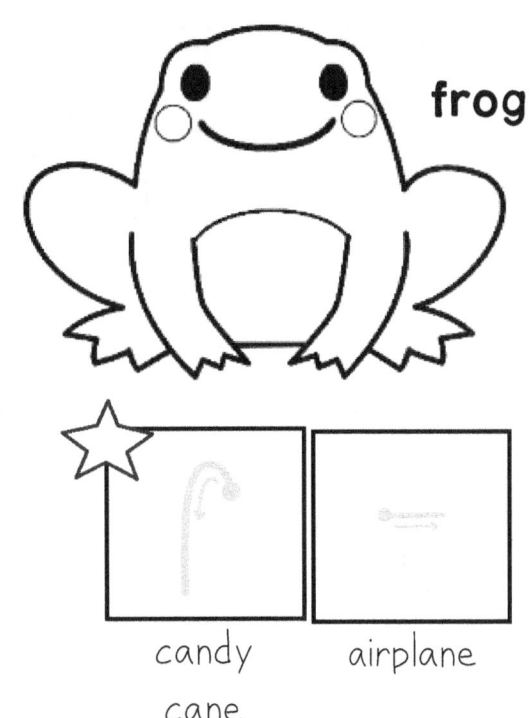

frog

candy cane   airplane

Hook

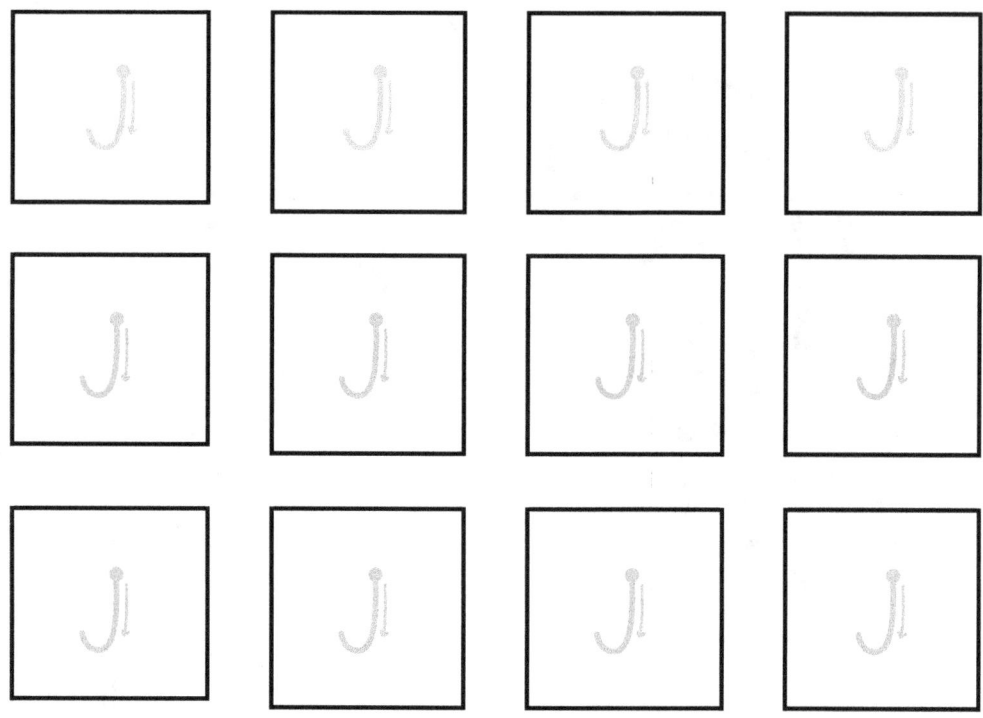

Catch the fish!

It is time to go fishing.

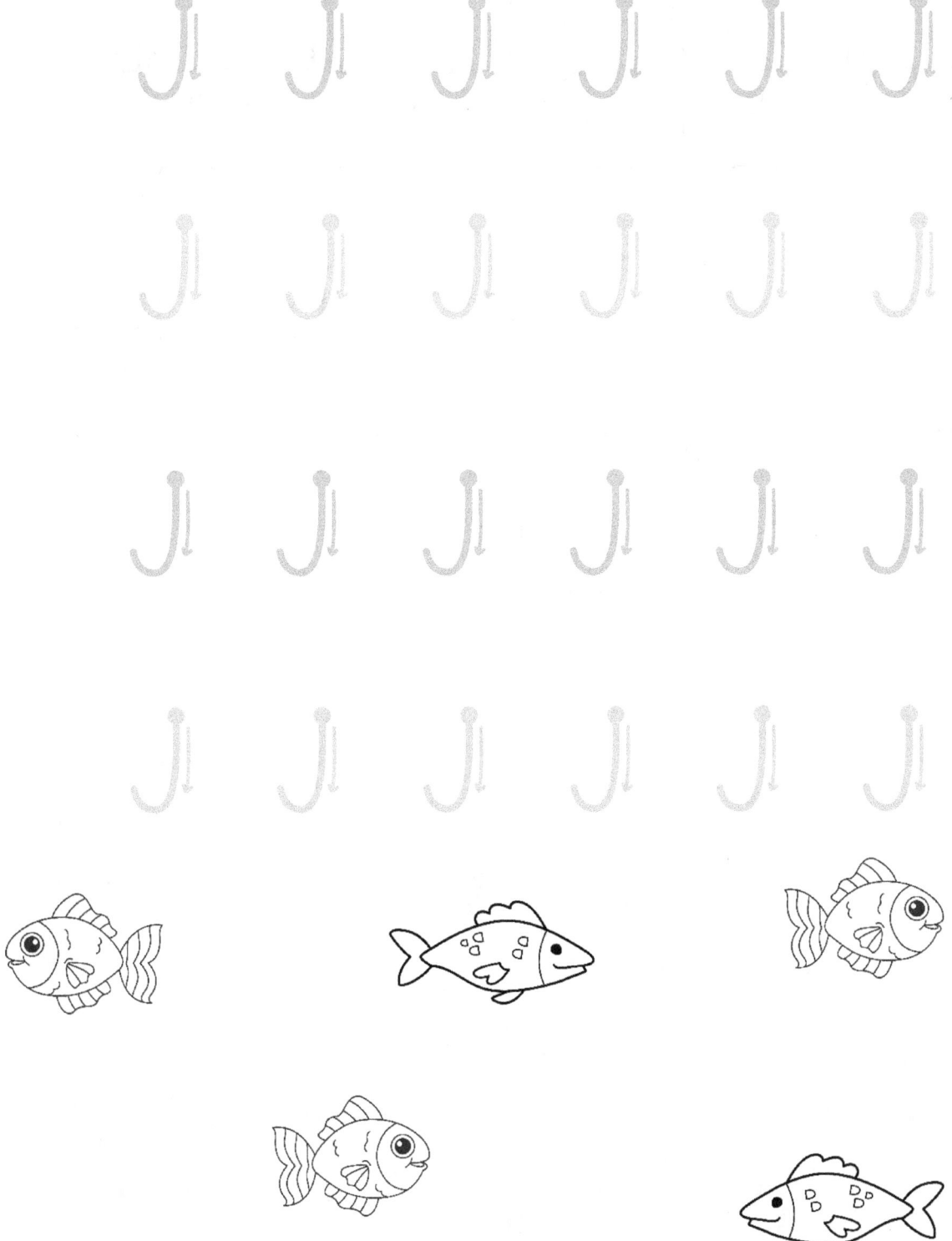

Draw your own writing patch.

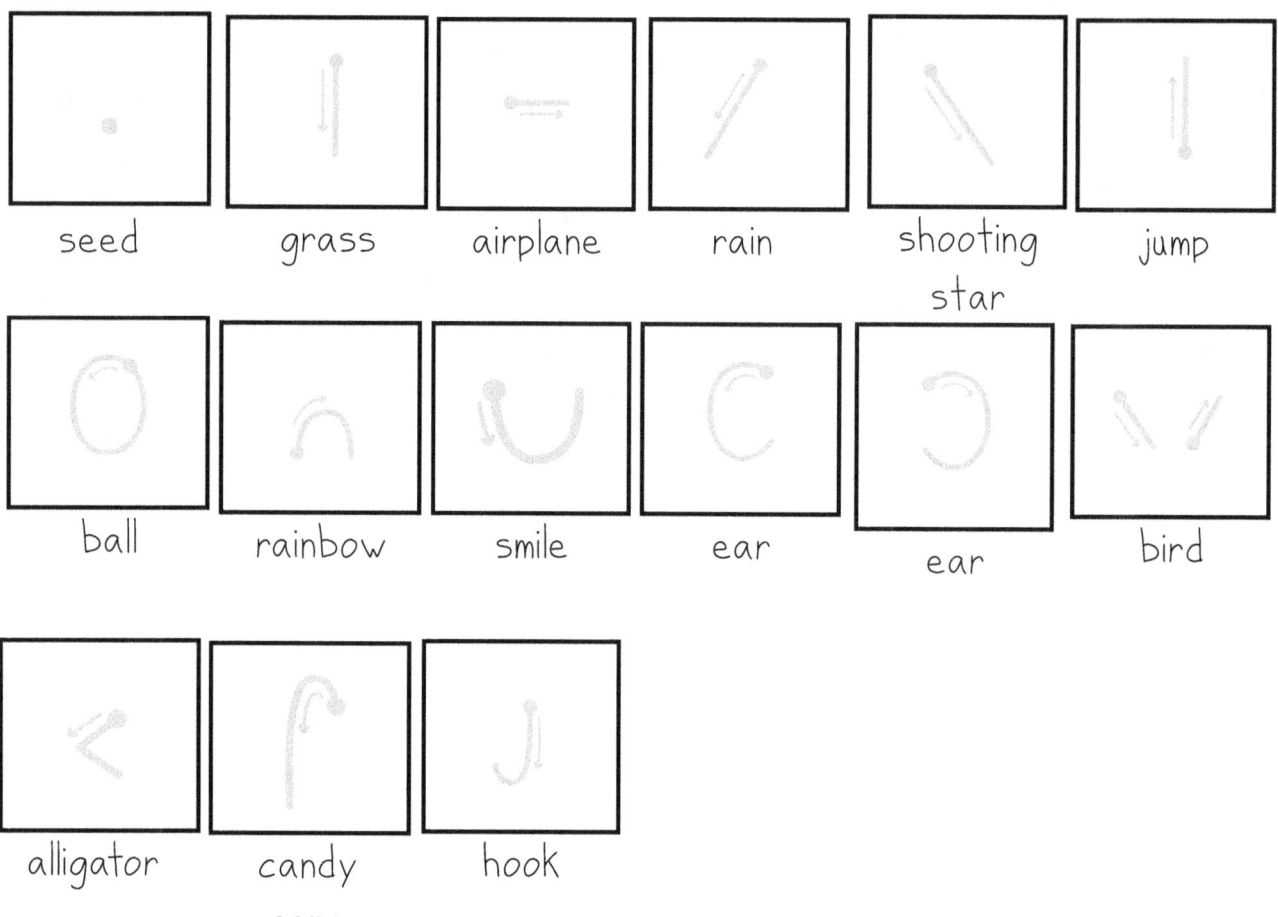

Letter j

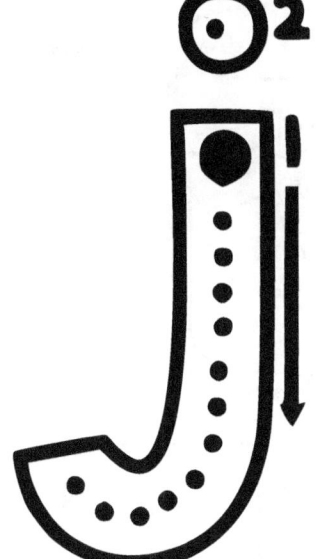

jam

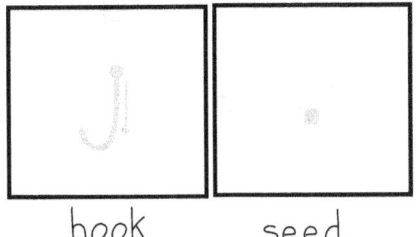

hook   seed

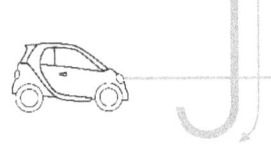 j   j   j   j

 j

☆
🚗 j

Letter J

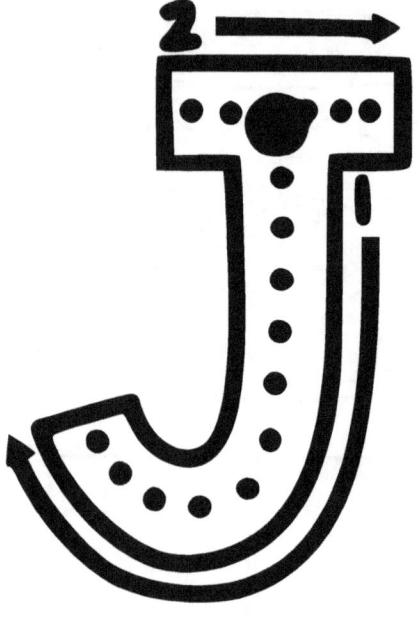

jam

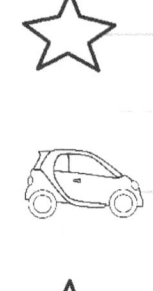

hook   airplane

Letter g

ghost

ball   hook

Make a boy.

Make a girl.

Turtle

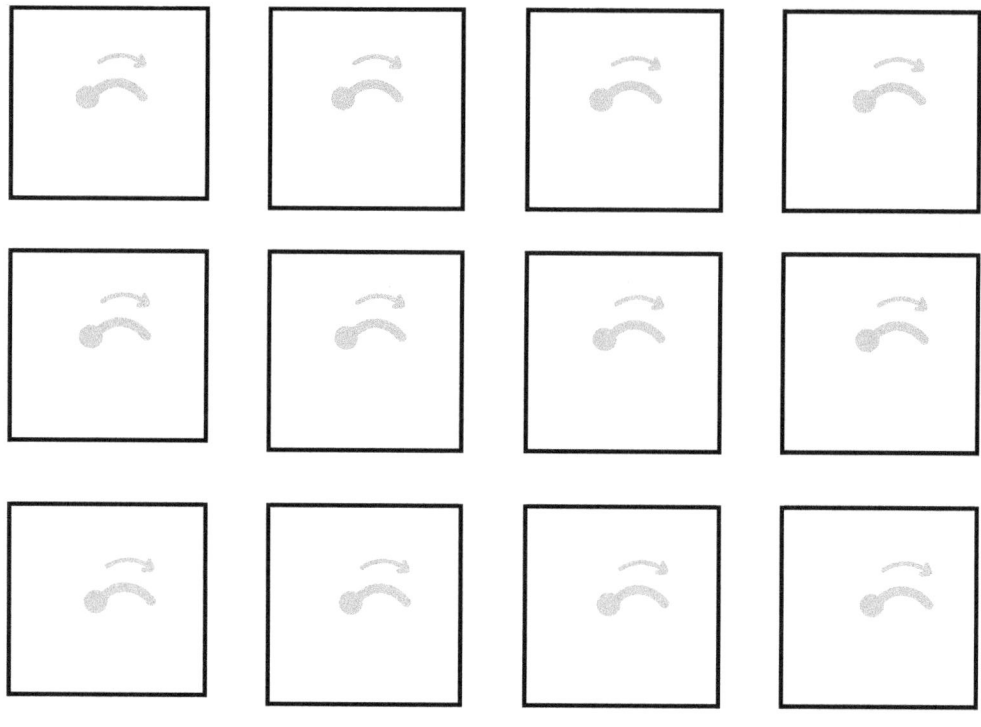

Here comes Turtle!

Draw your own writing patch.

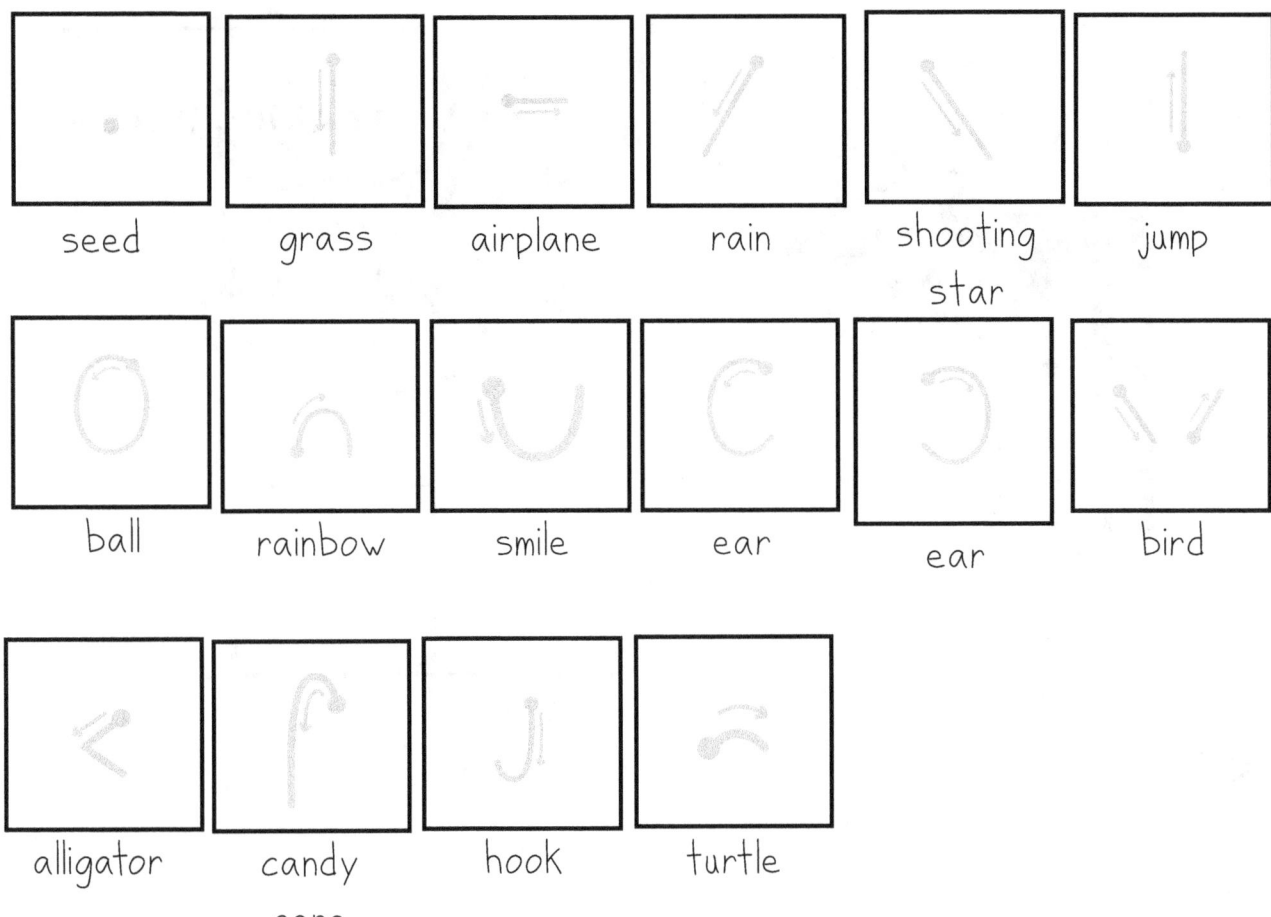

Letter r

rocking horse

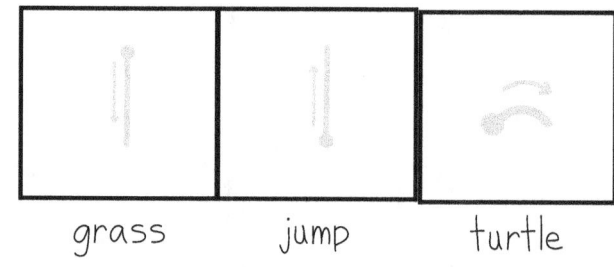

grass   jump   turtle

Snake

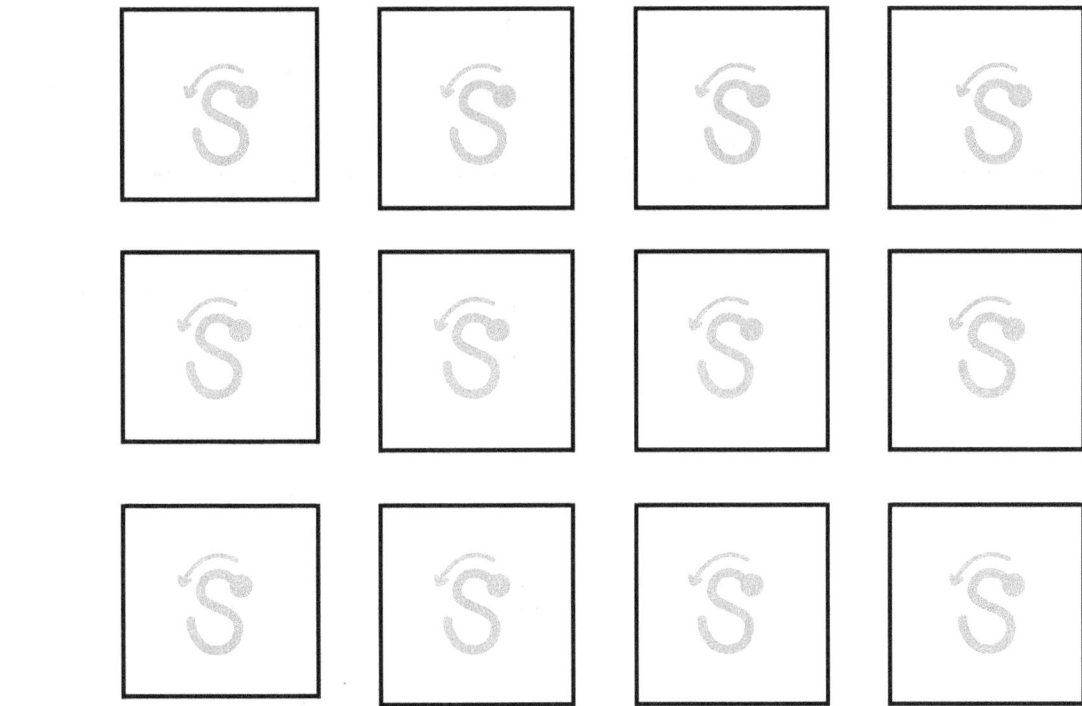

Watch out for the snake!

Draw your own writing patch.

Letter S

Snail

snake

  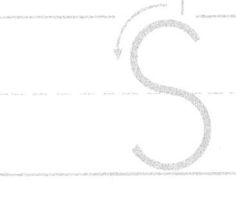 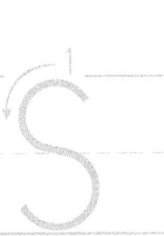 

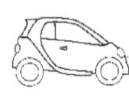

Letter s

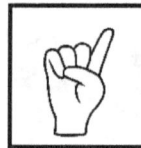  

snail

snake

The Writing Patch!

Make your own writing patch!

Number 0

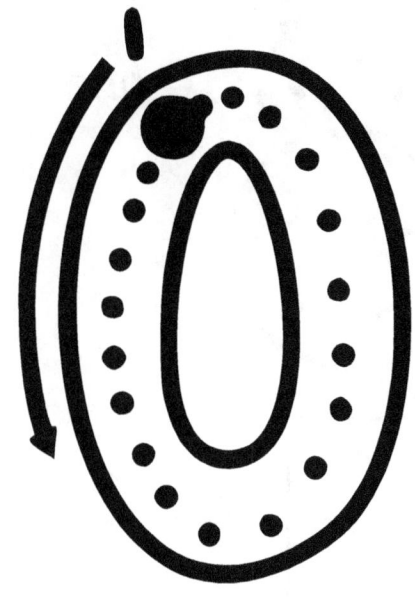

ball

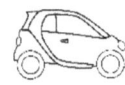

Number 1

one

grass

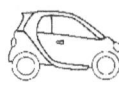

Number 2

two

ear airplane

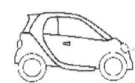

Number 3

three

ear　ear

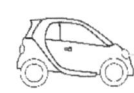

Number 4

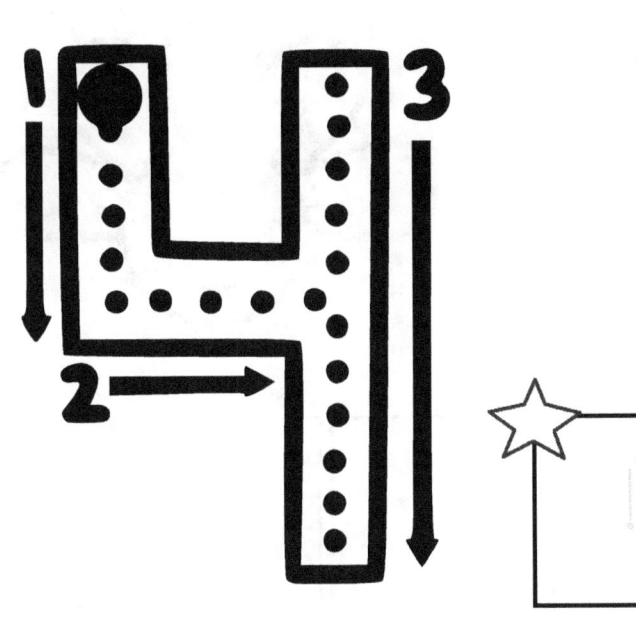

four

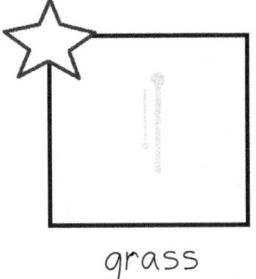  
grass   airplane   grass

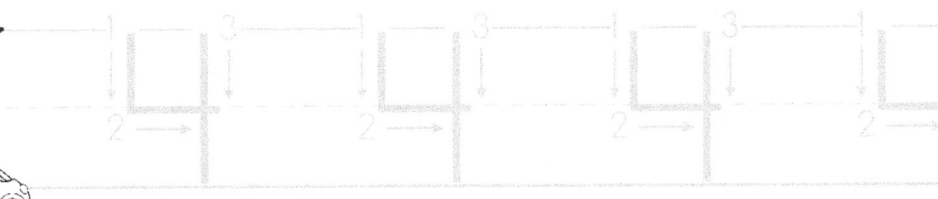

 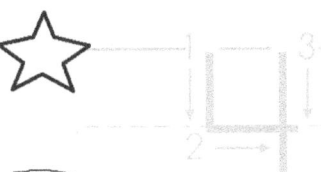

Number 5

five

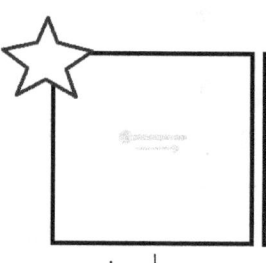  

airplane   grass   ear

Number 6

six

rain ball

Number 7

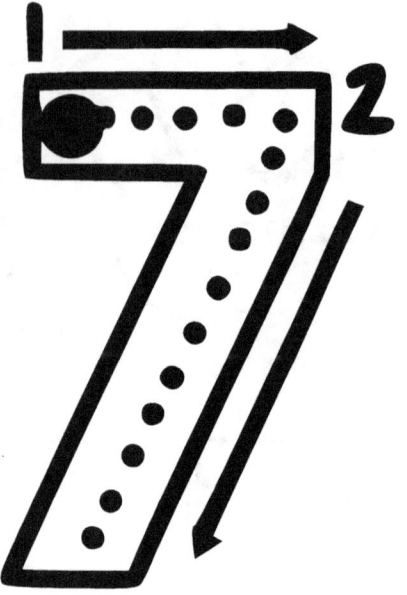

seven

airplane   rain

Number 8

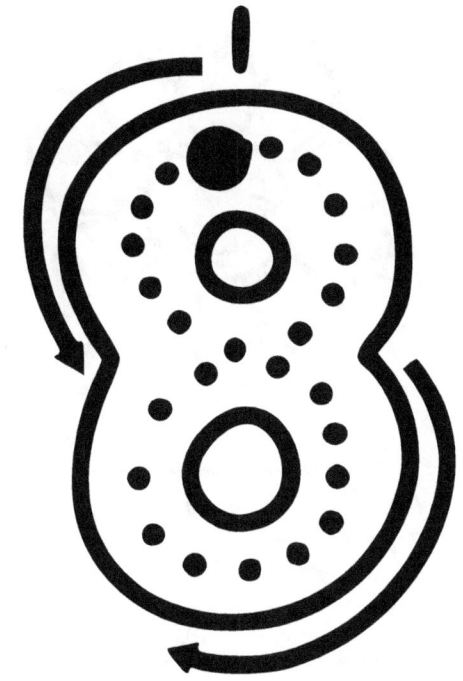

eight

snake   rain

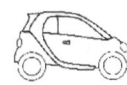

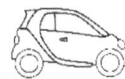

Number 9

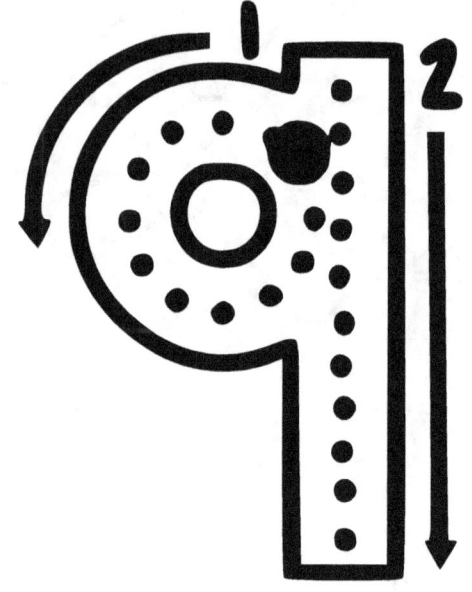

nine

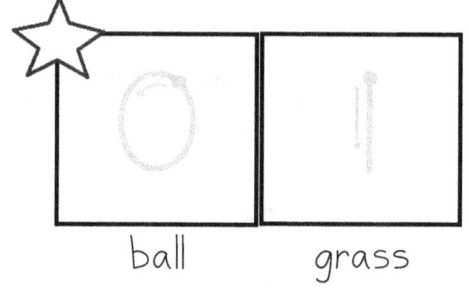
ball grass

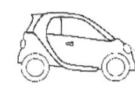

Number 10

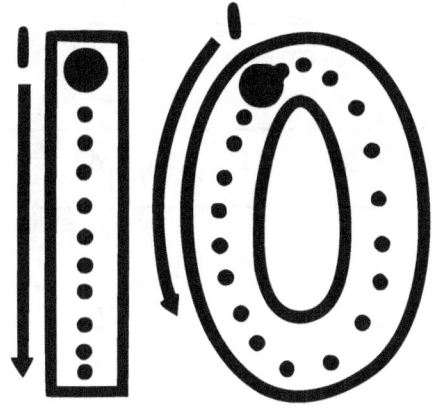

ten

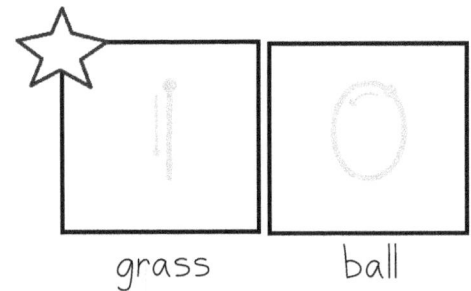
grass   ball

Introduction	3		Letter X	40
Writing Left to Right	5		Letter y	42
Driving left to right	6		Letter Y	43
Large motor multi-sensory directions	7		Jump	44
Seed	9		Letter N	47
Grass	13		Letter b	49
Star intro	16		Letter o	52
Letter l	18		Letter O	53
Letter I	21		Letter a	54
Airplane	23		Letter q	55
Letter t	26		Letter Q	56
Letter T	27		Sun	57
Letter L	28		Rainbow	62
Letter E	29		Letter n	65
Letter F	30		Letter h	66
Letter H	31		Letter m	67
Letter I	32		Smile	68
Rain	33		Letter U	71
Shooting Star	36		Letter u	72
Letter A	39		Ears	76
Letter x	40		Letter c	80

Letter C	81		Candy Cane	108
Letter e	82		Letter f	111
Letter G	83		Hook	112
Letter d	84		Letter j	115
Letter D	85		Letter J	116
Letter b	86		Letter g	117
Letter B	87		Letter r	122
Letter p	88		Snake	123
Letter P	89		Letter s	125
Letter R	90		Letter S	126
Bird	92		Number 0	129
Letter v	96		Number 1	130
Letter V	97		Number 2	131
Letter w	98		Number 3	132
Letter W	99		Number 4	133
Letter M	100		Number 5	134
Alligator	101		Number 6	135
Letter k	104		Number 7	136
Letter K	105		Number 8	137
Letter z	106		Number 9	138
Letter Z	107		Number 10	139

Help your new or struggling reader at

Reading-Patch.com

Thank you to our illustrators

Mrs. Stanford's Class

www.ingramcontent.com/pod-product-compliance
Lightning Source LLC
Chambersburg PA
CBHW081155290426
44108CB00018B/2562